Quilting
THROUGH LIFE

with JENNY
DOAN

Quilting

THROUGH LIFE

with JENNY
DOAN

PATTERNS
AND PROSE
FOR EVERY
STAGE OF LIFE

Jenny Doan

with Hillary Doan Sperry

HARPER HORIZON

Published by Harper Horizon, an imprint of HarperCollins Focus LLC.

Any internet addresses, phone numbers, or company or product information printed in this book are offered as a resource and are not intended in any way to be or to imply an endorsement by Harper Horizon, nor does Harper Horizon vouch for the existence, content, or services of these sites, phone numbers, companies, or products beyond the life of this book.

Executive Editor: Jenny Doan
Writing: Jenny Doan, Hillary Doan Sperry
Creative Team: Jenny Doan, Natalie Earnheart, Misty Doan, Christine Ricks
Photography: Mike Brunner, Lauren Dorton, Jennifer Dowling, Dustin Wean
Sewist Team: Jenny Doan, Natalie Earnheart, Misty Doan, Courtenay Hughes, Carol Henderson, Janice Richardson
Interior Typesetting: Kait Lamphere

Contact Us
    Missouri Star Quilt Company
    114 N. Davis St.
    Hamilton, MO 64644
    888-571-1122
    info@missouriquiltco.com

ISBN 978-1-4002-4853-7 (ePub)
ISBN 978-0-7852-5309-9 (HC)

Library of Congress Control Number: 2023950908

Printed in Malaysia
24 25 26 27 28 COS 5 4 3 2 1

CONTENTS

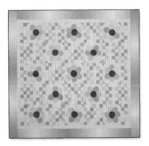

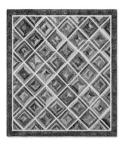
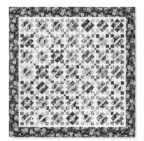

INTRODUCTION

My name is Jenny Doan. I'm a quilter and a creator. I've worked hard all my life to live happily. Somewhere along the line, I learned a little secret: happiness doesn't just happen. You choose it.

Happiness comes from being grateful every day. And when you aren't feeling it, you work to find things to be grateful for and to be happy about. It takes conscious effort, in every stage of life.

I tried to keep that happiness in our home and teach my children to live happily. There's a good chance you'll see some of that in this book. It's a great feeling. Quilting spreads happiness. Maybe not every time—some projects refuse to go smoothly—but if we can give ourselves space to make mistakes, learning to quilt can happen quickly, expanding that happiness faster and further than we realize.

I made plenty of mistakes when I was learning to quilt and even when I started filming videos. I'm the kind of girl who doesn't read the instructions on a new project. I pull out all the parts and look at it to see if I can put it together; if I can't, then I go to the instructions. And I wing it.

That should have been my first clue that I see instructions and patterns differently than others. When I started quilting, I surprised a lot of people. I streamlined patterns to fit my easygoing way of quilting and found simpler ways to do things. Apparently, I don't quilt the way others do.

Making quilting videos was no different. I wasn't your standard quilter, and people noticed right away. I taught quilting the way I wanted to, with excitement and passion. It didn't occur to me to be anything but authentic. I cut, sewed, and put blocks together with as many shortcuts as I could find. I used every scrap of fabric, and I made mistakes, misspoke, or had to redo things. And trust me, those first videos we made were very . . . authentic.

Somehow, those mistake-riddled videos helped me

connect with a lot of people. They humanized a complex craft and made it attainable. The art of quilting allows us to express how we feel, create something beautiful, and extend the warmth in our hearts to wrap around those we love.

With all our mistakes—and possibly because of them—quilts tell the stories of time. They mark the passage of seasons and years, acknowledging the important stages of our lives. Each stitch is a symbol of moments and memories, from the handmade blanket that swaddles a newborn to the quilt that comforts a grieving family member.

I've cried into quilts with brokenhearted friends and daughters and wrapped up icy adventurers as my sons came in from their winter escapades with half-frozen toes. These moments are the real reason we give and gather quilts. Quilts remember our history and carry it forward. They strengthen and soften our hearts, touching lives as we share our craft.

Quilts fill our homes with comfort, compassion, and unity. Quilts absorb the tears that fall and capture the laughter that brings us together. As soon as I send a quilt out into the world, it starts a whole new life. The quilts I've created are still out there, building memories with new families.

I didn't learn to quilt until years after I'd become a grandma for the first time, and I wish I'd started sooner. I don't really have regrets in my life, but quilting has brought me so much joy. If I can share that joy with you, it makes us both better.

This book will take you through many significant events from my life. Milestones and momentous occasions that affected my heart. These usually came as life changes. As most people do, we often fight change, probably without even realizing it, but change brings new experiences. As quilters we see these milestones as a chance for us to show how much we care. The mutual experiences of our lives are strengthened with the quilts we create and share. You don't have to be a quilter to enjoy the stories I share along with these events. My hope is that you'll come out feeling less alone and excited to try some of the ideas that have inspired you.

Creativity strengthens us, and quilting puts a purpose behind our craft. Whether this is your first trek into quilting or you're a seasoned sewist with a closet full of quilted histories, this art will change you in ways you never expected.

We come to quilting from a variety of places, but we stay because it makes us better. Fabric and quilting will change you. For me it is so much more than a craft. My first quilt came to me as a gift when I was a young child. My mother didn't sew, but she wanted me to have something to wrap my baby dolls in. So she had a friend make me a small quilt that consisted of four multicolored star blocks, pieced into a bright red background and sashed with pink-and-green speckled borders. It became my first heirloom quilt, and I still treasure it.

Within these pages, you'll find some of my favorite patterns for quilts that help or represent many of the important milestones of our lives. I hope you enjoy these projects as much as I have. Each pattern has detailed instructions, so you'll be able to create it from start to finish.

Quilting Through Life isn't just a book of patterns and stories; it's an opportunity to understand the ways that quilts have impacted and will continue to impact your most profound moments.

HOW TO CREATE A QUILT: STEP BY STEP

Commemorating life's special moments with handmade quilts is an incredibly rewarding hobby. It all starts with choosing your fabrics and selecting a pattern that will resonate with timeless elegance. The projects in this book will help you celebrate new life, honor a family member, commemorate a changing season, and so much more. They are designed to suit a variety of skill levels, including those of both new quilters and seasoned pros. By following along with the patterns, you can create a variety of quilts using traditional and contemporary styles of patchwork.

Before you start quilting, I want to share some of my tips and tricks for success. There is so much to learn from each step in the process, from measuring and cutting to quilting and binding. First-time quilters may want to come back to this section a few times for pointers as they stitch up their creations.

Cutting Fabric

There are some wonderful tools available for cutting fabric, and I know you'll appreciate how much easier they make the task of quilting for a loved one.

- I recommend that quilters invest in and use a good rotary cutter (a 45-mm size should do the trick) and a few extra blades to swap in when your current one gets dull. And don't forget to close that blade when you're done cutting to avoid any mishaps in the sewing room.

- Next, you'll want to pick up an acrylic ruler. It's a good idea to get a 6" x 24" size for cutting yardage, though a smaller size like 5" x 15" or 2.5" x 8" will work for slicing up precuts.
- Finally, you'll want a self-healing cutting mat. A large 36" x 24" mat will be useful for a variety of projects, but a smaller mat is perfectly fine to get you started.

To cut fabric with a rotary cutter, place your cutting mat on a desk or table. You'll likely be standing here for a few minutes, so choose a comfortable height.

TIP: Try not to sit while cutting, because you'll need that extra pressure and accuracy that comes with slicing fabric from directly overhead.

Take a look at the grid lines on your cutting mat and ruler. They will help you line up your fabric as you cut to get nice, straight lines. For safety's sake, always hold the rotary cutter close to your body and cut in the opposite direction away from where you're standing. Use steady pressure and hold the ruler firmly with your nondominant hand while cutting, keeping your fingers out of the way of the blade.

To ensure that your cutting mat lasts as long as possible without warping, never iron fabric on it. Also, keep it away from warm places like heater vents and windows. Changing your blade often can also help extend the life of your mat.

Sewing

After the fabrics are cut, it's time to head to the sewing machine. I recommend putting in a fresh 80/12 universal quilting needle before starting a new project or after about eight hours of sewing. This will help you avoid skipped stitches and other inconsistencies. Also, make sure you're using quality thread. A new 50-weight cotton thread will give you the best results when putting blocks together.

TIP: Try not to worry too much about getting the perfect ¼" seam. If you use a consistent seam allowance the whole time you're sewing blocks, everything will line up just fine.

We'll be using a ¼″ seam for all the projects throughout this book. Some sewing machines come with a ¼″ foot to help you keep a consistent seam allowance. If you don't have one of these handy feet, a piece of tape or a seam guide can help you stay on track.

Pressing, Trimming, and Squaring

The first step in getting your quilt blocks ready to join together is to press the seams. We recommend pressing seams toward whichever side is darker when possible so they aren't visible through lighter fabrics.

> **TIP:** If you don't have a square ruler, you can line up diagonal seams on your block with a 45-degree mark on your long ruler before trimming off that extra little bit of fabric.

After the blocks are pressed, it's time to trim the edges. This is called *squaring up a block.* Square-shaped rulers are available in different sizes to help with this task, and they can be especially helpful for half-square triangles, as seen in the *Opposites Attract* pattern on page 73 and the *Pinwheel Picnic* pattern on page 87.

Squaring up your blocks will help them sit nice and even when joined into rows. As you sew blocks together into rows, I recommend *nesting* the seams together. To do this, press one row of seams to the right and the next row of seams to the left. To join the rows, pin or clip them together at the seams. They should sew together snugly, creating less bulk.

After the last row is pieced together, you've completed your quilt top. Press the quilt top, using some spray starch if you want to make it extra flat. Then trim and square up the entire top with a rotary cutter and the largest ruler you can find.

Backing

After your quilt top is pressed and trimmed, it's time to prepare your fabric backing. Measure the length and width of your quilt top, adding an extra 8″ to both the length and width of your quilt if it's going to be machine quilted. You can piece together 42″-wide yardage to get the size you need or use 108″-wide backing fabric for larger projects.

To piece the backing, first trim off all selvages and use a ½″ seam allowance to join the sections. Then sew the pieces together along the long edge. I like to press this seam allowance open, rather than to one side, to reduce the bulk. For small quilts (under 60″ wide), I place this backing seam horizontally on the quilt, but I use vertical seams for larger quilts. If you're using a print with a directional fabric, feel free to throw these rules out the window and position the fabric in the way that makes sense with the front of your quilt.

Batting, Thread, and Quilting

Even though you won't see the batting in your finished quilt, you'll be able to feel its comfort and warmth. I recommend cotton batting, which has a great feel and is easy to work with. Another good option is an 80/20 cotton-polyester blend batting, which has a nice drape. Both will complement your quilting design and will stand up well to many washes.

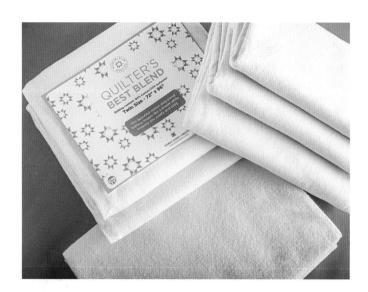

When choosing thread for quilting, a forgiving option for new quilters is to blend their thread color with the background of the quilt top. White, off-white, or gray thread can blend well with many fabrics. If your backing fabric is dark, you can use a darker thread in the bobbin and feed a lighter thread through the needle and machine. However, there are no rules when it comes to thread color, so feel free to be as bold as you'd like.

Basting is the process where you temporarily attach the three layers of the quilt—top, batting, and backing—together. Smooth out the layers and baste them together with basting spray or safety pins (placed every few inches) before quilting. This ensures that the layers do not shift during machine quilting. If you plan to send your quilt to a longarmer, you can skip this step altogether.

There are countless quilting designs you can choose from, from free-motion machine stippling to straight-line quilting. Beginners may want to stitch in the ditch (sew directly on the major seams) to hide the thread or disregard the seams altogether and choose an all-over pattern like swirls or wavy lines. The latter can actually help hide errors in piecing.

Binding

After you've quilted your project and trimmed off the excess batting and backing, it's time to finish your quilt with binding. Binding comes ready made, or you can create your own from yardage. I like to make binding from 2 1/2" jelly roll strips because it's already cut and ready to sew. You can choose a fabric that's featured in the quilt top or a coordinating color for this step.

Each project in the book has yardage listed for making your own binding. To make straight-grain binding, cut 2 1/2" strips of fabric straight across the width of the fabric (through the selvages). To make bias binding, cut the 2 1/2" strips on a 45° angle to get the maximum stretch. This is useful for going around corners.

Joining Strips: Plus-Sign Method

To join binding strips together, lay one strip across the other with the right sides together, like a plus sign. Stitch from the top inside to the bottom outside corners, crossing the intersections of fabric as you sew. Trim the seam to 1/4" and press the center seam open to reduce bulk.

Join as many strips together as you need to equal the perimeter of the quilt (the sum of all the edges) plus about 15" to 20" more to finish. The last step is to press the long strip in half widthwise to hide those seams, and then you're ready to start binding your quilt. See Construction Basics on page 182 for complete instructions on joining binding strips together.

Machine Binding

There are many ways to bind a quilt, but I prefer to machine stitch it to the front of my quilt, then use an invisible slip stitch to hand sew it to the back. A 1/4" seam allowance does the trick, as does leaving a 10" binding tail at the beginning and the end. Rather than starting the binding in a corner, I recommend starting off in the middle of one long edge.

Mitered Corners

Stop sewing about 1/4" from the corner and take a backstitch. Remove the quilt from under the presser foot and clip your threads. Flip the binding up at a 90° angle to the edge just sewn, making a tiny triangle. The tail of the binding should point straight up. Then, fold the binding back down from the top edge, right next to the side that will be sewn next, aligning the raw edges. Sew from the top fold down on the next side, doing a little backstitch right at

the beginning. This is how you can make perfect mitered corners every time. See Construction Basics on page 183 for complete instructions on binding around the corners of a quilt.

Closing the Binding

When your needle is 12″ away from the starting point, stop sewing! Remember those 10″ binding tails we left at both ends? Lay them atop each other and press a crease at their meeting point. Fold back the extra, measuring just 2 ½″ of overlap. Trim off the rest of the binding strip and set it aside.

Use the plus-sign method to match the edges and pin in place. Use a pencil or washable pen to mark your sewing line, and stitch a straight line from the top inside corner to the bottom outside corner. After you press the seam open and fold the entire section of binding in half, it should rest neatly against the edge of your quilt. Stitch the binding down to the front side of your quilt, flip the edge over to the back side, and tack it in place with an invisible stitch or machine stitch. See Construction Basics on page 183 for complete instructions on finishing your quilt binding.

CHAPTER 1

BABIES

Picture a newborn baby. Fragile fingers, tiny toes, wrinkled skin, sweet little nose, and vocal cords that can outdo a powerful rendition of a bugle wake-up call. Through that precious wail, picture the baby's mother. She's exhausted, sore, and smiling. Or maybe she's groggy from surgery. Perhaps she's a first-time mom and has no idea what to do with this tiny, shrieking child. Or she's waited years to finally hold her little one and tears up when she hears her infant's cry. Whether she carried her child or they came into her life in another beautiful way, the love a mother feels for her child is fierce. When she holds that baby close, it's all worth it.

There's a playfulness that comes with the baby stage, you know. They're miraculous, and I could never believe that my body could make a being like that. I'd hold each of my newborn children in my arms, in awe at this creation. I think I will always miss the feeling of babies growing inside me and anticipating the life they'll have.

I was told I would never have children. Are you surprised? I was. I've always wanted to be a mother. Many women of my age weren't taught to want anything besides motherhood. Even so, being a mother was the greatest ambition of my life. I had many passions and was never afraid to fight for them, but when the challenges of my body made the doctors believe I would never be able to have this one thing I wanted most, it shattered me.

The Doan Gang! Boys pictured on the left: Darrel in the back, then Ron, with Al in the black checkered shirt, Josh in red, and Jake in stripes at the front. Girls pictured on the right: Natalie in the back, then Jenny, with Sarah beside her and Hillary to the very right.

I'd love to tell you of some secret success or magic treatment I happened upon, but the truth is I was lucky. I did all I knew how to do—then prayed and pushed forward in my world. After multiple miscarriages, I finally had my first baby girl, Natalie. I made her tiny clothes and bibs and blankets. I even made an embroidered wall hanging in the fabulous neon greens, pinks, and oranges of the seventies. My nonsewing mother made her one as well—almost. My mother's embroidery wasn't finished until Natalie was getting married, but it made the gift all the more precious.

The quilts my children received were from friends, kind and generous quilters who taught me that a child has two great loves. Their first love is their mother, and their second is their blanket.

Children become so attached to their blankets. They're an appendage of the child, carried everywhere they go. More than any other quilt, baby quilts are expected to be well used and worn. They bring the old saying "Use it up, wear it out, make it do, or do without" to vivid life. While children rarely have to do without their beloved blankets, the tears of a child drive most parents to climb mountains and swim oceans to find a favorite belonging or comfort item, if it's been left behind. Children will use their quilts until they become threadbare fabric scraps dragging behind them. Even after suffering tantrums that lasted throughout the morning, seeing my little one tucked under a quilt, peacefully sleeping, always made my heart swell.

Baby quilts are lifelong treasures. They are used, loved, and worn to shreds. When you look at your own well-loved baby blanket, it tugs at your emotions. You hold it to your face and feel the soft comfort worn into that precious arrangement of childlike fabric. When I was a toddler, I had a miniature quilt with large, bold, red stars pieced into each corner. I adored it, slept with it, tucked it under my chin, and dragged it all over the house until the edges frayed. I wrapped my dolls in it and pretended it was a cape, a tent, and so much more. Quilts are filled with magic!

Ron and his daughters.

One of my daughters had a yellow checked quilt that my mother and I tied for her. It wasn't made to be fancy; it was made to be loved, like my own childhood blanket. She dragged it with her until she'd worn holes through both sides of the fabric and pulled, chewed, and twisted the yarn tails on the ties until they felted into tiny knots. But what did it matter? There's an instinct these days to protect beloved toys and clothes, to preserve and keep them in brand-new quality. That little girl didn't care! It was her blanket. I make a point of telling young parents that these quilts are not for show. They should be used, loved, and worn out.

The first quilt children receive blesses not only them but their mother as well. It brings comfort and quiet to the home of a sleepless baby. Baby quilts may be the most gratifying to give because you're almost guaranteed that the quilt will be loved as deeply as you love the recipient.

If quilting was all motherhood ever asked of us, we could stop the chapter here, and it would be all baby smiles and laughter. But the reality of motherhood was different than what I thought it would be.

All my life I had wanted to be a mother. I imagined motherhood as walking through grassy fields in a long, flowing dress with dancing flowers at my feet and holding a lovely little baby. The baby was, of course, not crying but cooing prettily in my arms. In reality, babies cry anytime they need anything—and typically you have no idea what they need. You're exhausted mentally and physically, and you spend your days trying to clean up after this little person who only eats, sleeps, and uses up diapers. When you're not taking care of your precious little diaper machine, you try and sneak in naps or lunch or a shower.

For me, sometimes that phase felt like it lasted for years. Sometimes it did. It was an unavoidable life swing that was a lot more work than I thought it would be.

I'd been married for a few years before I had my first baby, and I thought I had things figured out. I wasn't prepared for how all-consuming that change would be. At first I loved it. I carried my little girl around and barely let anyone else hold her. I was convinced I was the only one who could mother her. After a week of barely sleeping, I loved it less. I was still the only one who could mother her, but I really just needed five minutes to rest.

It didn't stay like that. I made it through my baby's first year of life and found I was pregnant with my second child, and it actually got more difficult. I realized at one point I hadn't changed my clothes in days, and I hadn't been alone in years, not even long enough to use the bathroom by myself.

I'm pretty sure that thought should have made me cry, but it didn't. I might have laughed, but I don't remember. Mostly I was numb.

I loved my babies, but this mother thing was hard. If you want to know what tough love really is, talk to a mother with two babies under two who is simultaneously changing diapers and wiping spit-up off her shoulder. That's tough love, just in reverse of how we usually think of it.

Motherhood is tough, but I think it was meant to be like that. Giving everything to those helpless little babies creates a bond. I wasn't ready for the work entailed in being a mother, but when I was able to admit how hard it was, I came to a realization: what I was doing as a mother was divine. These precious children would die without me. Even changing diapers was a holy mission—if I didn't change their diaper they would literally die of disease. It changed my perspective, and every difficult, smelly, and not-so-enjoyable task became a divine, lifesaving act. Every day I served my babies and gave them my heart.

For a long time I tried to keep doing it all. I'd always been able to do everything. And I liked being that person. As much as I loved my children, I still loved being important in the other parts of my life. Yet I could feel that I needed to give myself over to motherhood, at least while they were so little. I didn't know if I could, but I had to, and I wouldn't make any other choice.

Eventually, I looked at myself in the mirror and said, "These little people are my life. I'm not gonna resent it. I'm not gonna be angry. This is what I do, until I don't. I'm the mom." It was enough to make the decision. Being a mom was still a hard job, but I stopped trying to pull myself in every direction. I could be the mom and know it was enough for me.

My children kept me going when times got tough. Knowing that I had these little people who depended on me, loved me, and needed me is what motivated me. Let's not nitpick the details.

A baby's years are such a small part of our lives. With baby after baby coming into my life, I had a flock of little people who for a long time thought I was magical. I loved that.

Ron, Jenny, Hillary, Al, Natalie, and Sarah at Easter.

Everyone needs to feel needed and wanted. We do so much for our kids, and they don't always find a way to return that caring. We know we love each other, but it's hard when we don't feel our love returned to us. When I was a young mother, I tried to do it all. For a long time, I did. After one of my younger sons was born, I had a bout of postpartum depression that knocked me flat. At the time, I didn't realize how bad it was. All I knew was that I wanted to lie in bed and not get out.

I cried and hid. My sweet husband became a buffer of love that stood between me and the world, though I couldn't always feel it. Ron would come home and take care of dinners, diaper changes, and cleaning . . . and deflecting the myriad of people who needed me. Depression is debilitating for an entire family, and mine bore a heavy load on my behalf, but that didn't change the weight of the pain and fear I was feeling.

Afterward, I reevaluated my priorities. Prior to that time in my life, I'd volunteered in the community, with theater, school groups, and church, and I would often answer every phone call with an easy yes. Now I put a note by the phone that said, "Let me think about that and call you back." Because, yes, I could do most of the things asked of me, but did I have the time? The capacity? I had to accept that I didn't have to do it all. In fact, I couldn't.

When I was a young mother, there was a poem that resonated with me as I struggled to find my limits. It talked about how dust and cobwebs could wait, and dishes and dirty floors weren't as important as rocking and loving my baby. I even had the last stanza embroidered and hung on my wall to remind me of the precious time I had with my babies. That poem gave me license to rest.

Even though I wasn't the kind of person to reach out and ask for help, there were a few people who saw what I needed and stepped in when I was running low on hands. There are (and will always be) an infinite number of things to be done in the house, but the time we have with our little ones is anything but infinite.

First Baby and Grandbaby

Welcoming a little one into your family is one of life's most precious moments. Suddenly, you're holding a new person in your arms, and you can't imagine your life without them. Now that I have grandchildren to look up at me with wide, innocent eyes, I have a whole new flock of little ones that clamor after me and think I'm grand. Like no time has passed, all the magic returns because now I'm Grandma.

When my oldest daughter was born, we didn't have much money. Baby boutiques and cute, coordinating baby gear were way out of our budget. On top of that, there was no such thing as sonograms. So, without any of those conveniences, we worked hard to set up a nursery for our new little one, not knowing whether our baby would be a boy or a girl. My husband and I made a sturdy wooden cradle, and I made bumpers and sheets and newborn clothes in yellows and greens for our prospective little boy or girl.

Taking the time to prepare a place for a new child is one of my favorite parts of having a baby. Painting the walls, setting up the crib, and decorating the room are all part of the process, but finally holding your little one is what it is all about.

By the time I started quilting, my children were having children. My granddaughter Hannah received the first baby quilt I ever made. It was not my first quilt, and I was no expert, but I made her a classic windmill quilt in pale florals. Shortly after that came a quilt for Katie, and then Olivia, and then came the boys. Pretty soon, grandchildren were coming like a flood, and I quickly gained a new appreciation for sweet and simple quilts.

Jenny, Ron and (some of) the grandkids!

Baby quilts are a great entry point into quilting. It's a project you can finish even if you only have a little sewing experience. Simple is usually better with a baby quilt, but even if you choose a pattern with more detail, you have to make that block only four times, not thirty-four times. That's why baby quilts make such good first projects.

A baby quilt is a gift that channels your love through the touch of fabric and warmth. When you finish, you accessorize that quilt with a beautiful little baby, and no matter what your skill level is, it's suddenly a treasure!

I now have twenty-seven grandchildren, and I was blessed to make baby quilts for almost all of them. The first few grandchildren came along before I was quilting, but I'm not one to play favorites—they got toddler quilts.

Every grandchild has a piece of my heart patterned into their quilt. These simple projects kick off a foundation of love and connection in my relationship with them, even when they are not as nearby as I'd like. Making baby quilts has been as much of a gift to me as it has been to them. When I began making quilts for my grandchildren, I had no idea how it would connect us. I held my grandbabies in the quilts I made for them, and as they grew, I made larger quilts and dress-up costumes. I mended skirts and pants and taught them how to do the same.

In the process of giving, we all gained so much more. I shared, they learned. They played, I laughed. It's become a never-ending cycle of loving each other, with quilts along the way.

BREEZY WINDMILLS
QUILT

*B*reezy Windmills is one of the first baby quilts I ever made. The windmill blocks are quick to piece with strip quilting, composing a fast and fabulous project to share. This pattern's staggered squares can come in a rainbow of colors or in dainty florals like I used when making it for my sweet granddaughter.

Baby quilts are for daily use. The designs don't have to be complicated since your time and effort will be tripled with the love and use this quilt will get. Plus, with the simplicity of the design, *Breezy Windmills* gives us the luxury of a fast and fun project catering to any quilt size or style.

Project Info

Quilt Size
85" x 93"

Block Size
8 ½" unfinished, 8" finished

Supply List

Quilt Top
1 roll of 2 ½" print strips
1 roll of 2 ½" background strips

Inner Border
¾ yard

Outer Border
1 ½ yards

Binding
¾ yard

Backing
8 ½ yards for vertical seam(s) or 3 yards of 108" wide

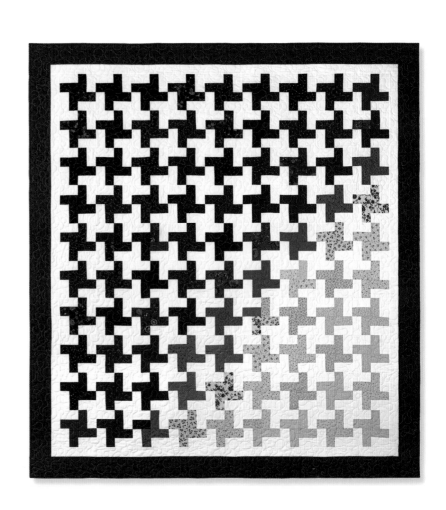

1 Make Strip Units

1A

Sew 1 print strip to 1 background strip, lengthwise. Open and press. **Make 40** strip sets.

Cut each strip set into (9) 4 ½″ strip units for a **total of 360**. **1A**

2 Block Construction

2A

Select 4 units with matching or similar color values. Arrange these in 2 rows of 2. Notice that the print sections of the units meet in the center. **2A**

Sew the units together in rows and press in opposite directions. Nest the seams and sew the rows together. Press. **2B**

As you continue to make blocks with matching or similar color values, you will have some units that do not have 4 matching or similar colors. Arrange 4 of these units so they will transition 1 color to the next in your gradient arrangement. Sew these together in the same manner as before. **Make 90** blocks. **2C**

Block Size: 8 ½″ unfinished, 8″ finished

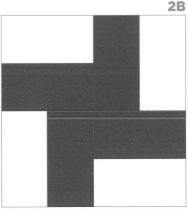

2B

3 Arrange and Sew

Lay out your blocks in **10 rows of 9 blocks**. Notice that the gradient layout transitions 1 color to the next. Sew the blocks together in rows. Press the seams in opposite directions. Nest the seams and sew the rows together. Press. **3A**

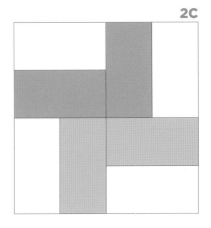

2C

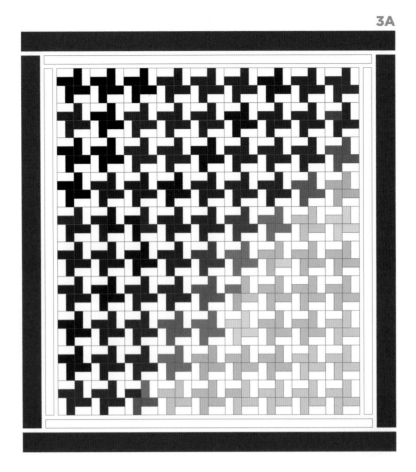

4 Inner Border

Cut (8) 2 1/2″ strips across the width of the inner border fabric. Sew the strips together to make one long strip. Trim the borders from this strip.

Refer to Borders (page 181) in the Construction Basics to measure, cut, and attach the borders. The lengths are approximately 80 1/2″ for the sides and 76 1/2″ for the top and bottom.

5 Outer Border

Cut (9) 5″ strips across the width of the outer border fabric. Sew the strips together to make one long strip. Trim the borders from this strip.

Refer to Borders (page 181) in the Construction Basics to measure, cut, and attach the borders. The lengths are approximately 84 1/2″ for the sides and 85 1/2″ for the top and bottom.

6 Quilt and Bind

Layer the quilt with batting and backing, then quilt. After the quilting is complete, square up the quilt and trim away all excess batting and backing. Add binding to complete the quilt. See Construction Basics (page 182) for binding instructions.

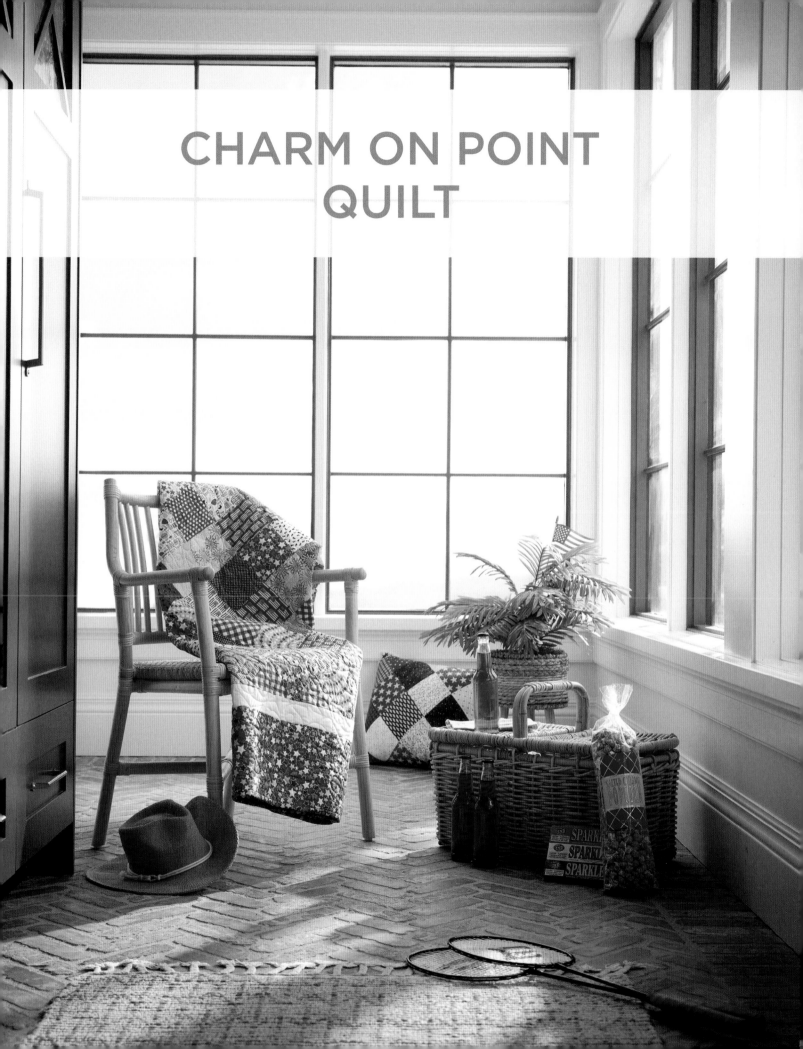

CHARM ON POINT QUILT

Because baby quilts are often the first quilts people attempt to make, it's best to keep it simple. *Charm On Point* is a great pattern for new quilters because you can make something amazing without too much difficulty. Starting with patchwork blocks is easy and always cute, but when you turn them on point, they become darling little diamonds. With minimal waste and a simple insider trick, this beginner-friendly pattern is the perfect way to get started. And the oohs and aahs as you finish are only the prelude to snuggling a brand-new member of the family in this precious and practical quilt.

Project Info

Quilt Size

57 ³/₄" x 57 ³/₄"

Supply List

Quilt Top

2 packages of 5" print squares

Inner Border

¹/₂ yard

Outer Border

1 ¹/₄ yards

Binding

³/₄ yard

Backing

3 ³/₄ yards for vertical seam(s)

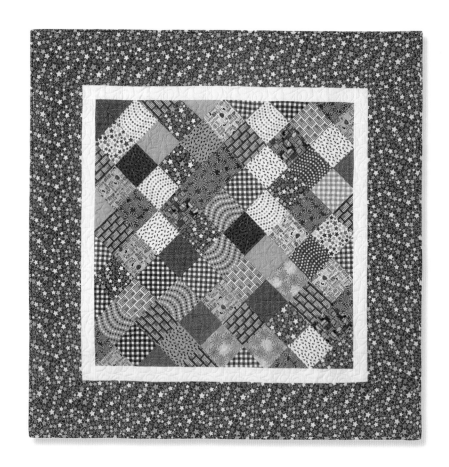

1 Sew

Sew the 5″ print squares into rows. Each row is made up of **6 blocks**, and you will need **12 rows**. While stitching the blocks together, mix up the color values so the lights, mediums, and darks are spread out rather than all grouped together. **1A**

Press the even rows toward the left and the odd rows toward the right so the seams will nest. Sew the rows together to make one large rectangle.

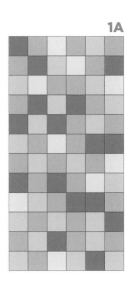

1A

2 Mark and Cut

Align a ruler with the upper right corner and the lower left corner of the bottom of the sixth row of squares. Make sure the ruler intersects the corner of each block. Cut on the diagonal, being careful not to stretch or tug on the edges. **2A**

Without moving the project, realign the ruler with the top of the first square on the left side of row 7 and the bottom of the last square on the right in row 12. Again, make sure the ruler is intersecting the corner of each block. Carefully cut on the diagonal.

Number each section, and draw an arrow beside the number so you can keep track of which direction each section is oriented. Refer to the diagram and notice how the sections are numbered. **2B**

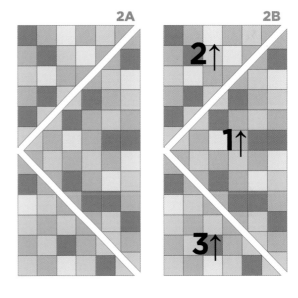

2A   2B

3 Arrange and Sew

Pick up Section 3 and place it to the right of Section 1. Make sure the arrows still point in the same direction as before. Pick up Section 2 and place it under Section 3. Refer to the diagram. **3A**

Sew Section 3 and Section 2 together horizontally. Press the seam allowances toward Section 2.

Add Section 1 to the left and sew in place after making sure all block seam allowances are aligned.

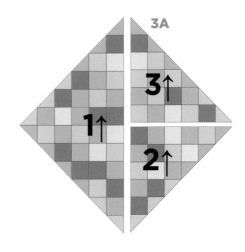

3A

4 Inner Border

Cut (5) 2 ½" strips across the width of the fabric. Sew the strips together end to end to make one long strip. Trim the borders from this strip. **4A**

Refer to Borders (page 181) in the Construction Basics to measure and cut the inner borders. The strips are approximately 39 ¼" for the sides and approximately 43 ¼" for the top and bottom.

4A

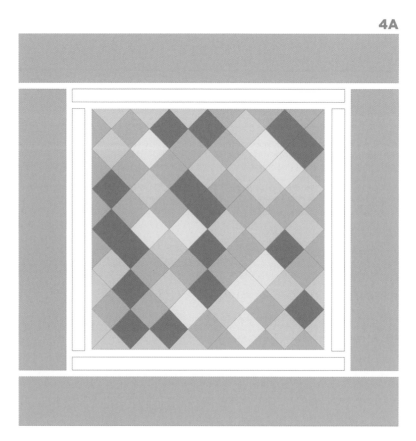

5 Outer Border

Cut (5) 8" strips across the width of the fabric. Sew the strips together end to end to make one long strip. Trim the borders from this strip.

Refer to Borders (page 181) in the Construction Basics to measure and cut the outer borders. The strips are approximately 43 ¼" for the sides and approximately 58 ¼" for the top and bottom.

6 Quilt and Bind

Layer the quilt with batting and backing, then quilt. After the quilting is complete, square up the quilt and trim away all excess batting and backing. Add binding to complete the quilt. See Construction Basics (page 182) for binding instructions.

CHAPTER 2

RAISING KIDS

I still remember the day I settled into the car and realized all my children were behind me in their seats—and I hadn't put them there. I sat there for a moment feeling like something was missing, like I'd forgotten something. We'd been busy, and when it was time to go, all I'd done was say, "All right, kids! Let's get in the car. It's time to go!"

And they went.

I turned around again and counted. They really were all there.

I hadn't needed to pack diapers or extra clothes. I didn't have to bring formula, snacks, or car toys. I didn't even have a diaper bag, for goodness' sake! I just got in the car, and they followed. It was this little, miraculous moment.

Raising my kids made up about half of my lifetime. As hard as it was, I chose it, and I loved it. From the time I saw my first baby's smile and held her tiny hand in mine until my youngest son packed up his quilt and kissed me goodbye as he left home, I've treasured being a mother. I never expected my children to stay little, you know, but seeing them grow, change, and need me less has been harder than I anticipated. As

Doan Kids from left to right: Darrel, Sarah, Hillary, Jake, Al, Natalie.

they go, I'm left with empty bedrooms and a staggered stack of quilts in graduating sizes to remind me of how far we've come. The leaving is inevitable, but thankfully, it's not the end of motherhood.

Children go from babies to toddlers to preteen youth, and still, they keep growing. Soon after, they become teenagers, needing larger, adult-sized quilts of their own. My boys grew so quickly, I'd regularly find them climbing in bed with a quilt pulled up over their chin—and their bare toes sticking out the bottom. They wouldn't always tell me when this happened, so I had to be vigilant and keep watch. This means there always had to be a new project on my machine if I wanted to keep them warm and covered.

I tried to hold these projects for the holidays, since our family makes the Christmas gifts we give to one another every year. Once, when we thought those growing boys had finally reached their peak height, Ron planned to make fleece blankets for everyone. He was so excited that the boys would finally have a blanket that covered their entire bodies. We got a deal on the fabric, and he managed to secretly measure those tall boys against his own height. Alan was the tallest, and when he opened his blanket Christmas morning, his smile lit up the room from the floor to the star on top of the tree. He opened every other gift while wrapped in that blanket and spent the day completely covered in fluffy fabric.

Jenny along with some of her grandkids: Ezra, Ashelyn, and Gideon.

Those gifts were blankets, not quilts, but both are heartfelt, tangible expressions of love. They wrap people up and touch lives. I've seen it over and over again. That Christmas, Alan's smile made all the secret plans and quiet work worth it. It was just a blanket, but it was a wonderful example of the joy of gift giving, proving that gifts will not only fill needs but touch hearts.

I gave my very first quilts to my oldest grandsons. I had taken a quilting class where we learned how to make a *Log Cabin* block. I was still afraid to step out of what I knew, but the pattern was fresh in my mind. So I duplicated what I'd learned, making three matching toddler quilts for my daughter Natalie's boys. They were identical down to the color of the fabric.

The boys were so excited about their quilts; they even loved that they matched. Within minutes of receiving them, the trio had disappeared, taking their quilts to their rooms. When Natalie and I found them later, they'd hung them from shelves and bedrails to play in their own little army of identical tents.

I kept learning, and my quilts took on a bigger importance for me as I shared them. It was exciting to create things for those little people I loved so much. The first time I heard about my grandkids moving their room around I got excited. Moving to a big-kid bed is a huge step in a child's life. In an effort to make them feel loved, I would sometimes help one of my grandchildren pick out special fabrics and a pattern to make a new quilt for their new bed.

When my kids were young, we couldn't afford to get new bedding every time they moved into a larger bed. We had the boys in one room and the girls in another. It was *cozy* in there. As they grew, we would periodically repaint and move things around in an attempt to redecorate. New quilts would have been nice, but rearranging made a big difference. It was a relatively simple way to help their rooms grow with them.

Even when we had very little, I tried to make each member of my family feel special.

We did the best we could with what we had. This often showed up at dinnertime. In fact, the less money we had, the fancier our dining became. We ate macaroni and cheese on china plates or grilled peanut-butter sandwiches by candlelight. Sometimes we only had enough in the budget for potatoes—I could get a ten-pound bag for seventy-nine cents—so I would fry up huge batches of french fries and set the table with fancy bowls full of ketchup, barbecue sauce, and any other dips we could think up. We called it a French Fry Bash. It was one of our family's favorite meals.

Doan kids in a wagon.

As an adult, Sarah came to me asking why no one else seemed to know about French Fry Bashes. It took me by surprise when she told me she wanted to start the tradition with her own family. I asked her, "Do you know why we had those dinners?"

"Of course," she said matter-of-factly. "Because they were fun!"

She had no idea we had French Fry Bashes because of our tight budget. That tradition was born out of necessity.

I was so grateful that she didn't see those times as scarce. I have been surprised over and over again at the ability a little creativity has to change our children's reality. We made our meals on a shoestring budget, but they were special because we made them special. We didn't cry over our lack; we used our creativity and made it grand. At least, that was my intention, and luckily, it came through in a way that was remembered with fondness.

It didn't matter how much I worried. I played with and cared for my babies to the best of my ability. Sometimes my best wasn't as good as it had been the day before, but I always gave everything I could. With my sweet husband at my side, it was always enough.

Our family went on adventures big and small, but at the end of the day, what the kids remembered wasn't the toys or clothes or food. What stayed with them were the moments: a sandcastle contest with a sibling on the beach, climbing a tree and finding a bird's nest, or getting to pick the direction and lead the way on a family walk.

Love was always the most important thing in our home, and there was always plenty of it to go around.

Don't get me wrong—we weren't perfect, by far. As my children grew, we had several mottos, such as "Work hard. Pray harder" and "Do a thing as best as you can and be happy for him who can do it better." But there was one in particular that came about because of a blanket.

Two of my girls were in the hall, arguing. For the life of me, I couldn't understand what had upset them. With both sets of hands wrapped around opposite ends of a blanket, they burst into tears. That blanket was the prize, their crown jewel, and the only thing that would get either of them to calm down.

Five generations of Doan women.

Taking a deep breath, I came between the tearful girls. "Girls, girls! Stop fighting, please!" My pleas did virtually nothing. Harsh words and accusations continued, and finally, I held up my hands, calling out, "It's just a blanket!"

My words finally got through to them. The fighting came to a stop, and silence settled over us.

I pulled each girl close and took the blanket. "This is your sister. Don't ruin your relationship over a blanket."

They looked at me with open mouths and wide eyes, but they eventually nodded. No matter the argument, they knew their relationship was more important than a blanket. They loved each other more than that.

"It's just a blanket" became a mantra in our home.

When passions rose and people got upset, someone would step in and remind the others, "It's just a blanket." Those four words would call us back and tell us that things are just things. Relationships will always be important. Love and people are what matter most.

Adventures and Hiking

My husband and I did the best we could while raising our kids. We wanted them to cherish their childhoods, with experiences and memories that outweighed their worries. Throughout their childhood years, we worked and played together. When the work was done, we went on adventures. It didn't matter if it was a holiday or just another Tuesday; we were very good at finding fun ways to spend time together. We took advantage of every moment, from "Penny Walks" around the block—where we reached the corner and flipped a coin to see if we continued right or left—to lazy afternoons on the beach and lively baseball games on summer evenings.

Quilts were part of many of those adventures. We always had one or two stashed in the car. Those quilts were our gathering place. We ate, read stories, and napped on them. While little ones traced patterns in the fabric or stuffed discovered treasures in the pockets of our big jean quilt, the others would play until they were tired and eventually found their way back to the quilt too.

Our favorite quilt was all denim squares. It was big enough to hold everyone on its heavy fabric top, and it went everywhere with us. It was great because it didn't attract grass or dirt; I could lay it out anywhere and fold it right back up into the car when we were done—unless someone had stuck sand in the pockets. Then it just took a quick shake, and all the debris fell out and brushed off, and we'd be good to go.

One of our greatest adventures was hiking in the mountains of Pinnacles National Park. We met up with some homeschooling friends to see rock formations and caves on a few short hikes. We did this several times, and each different hike and natural wonder enthralled my children.

Then one day, we decided to hike the whole trail. We loaded our backpacks with snacks and water and started out on another adventure.

It was simple and familiar at first. We hiked through caves and low ground trails, then up around boulders to stay on the path. Soon, the trail wasn't familiar at all, but others were hiking alongside us, so we kept going. My youngest was only five or six years old, and while I held his hand at the back of the pack, the older preteens pressed ahead. The sun rose higher, and the hike got longer, and I started to question what I'd signed us up for. But we were already in the mountains, and going back would take longer than going forward, so we kept moving.

By the time we were climbing the final stretch up the backs of the mountain peaks, we were completely worn out. One of my little red-faced daughters looked up at me while her siblings rallied ahead. "Mommy, I'm so tired," she said. I could see the exhaustion in her face, but I was already carrying my littlest.

"We're almost there. See?" I showed her the map. We really were only one climb away from the summit, but I didn't know how much of the map she understood. "You can do it. Just don't stop. You don't want to sleep here, do you?"

My teasing brought out her smile, and she shook her head. "Can we pray for help to make it to the top?"

I tell you what, we knelt down right there on the trail and prayed. My heart melted as her sweet voice carried strength and faith that I didn't know I'd taught her. Then we stood up and forged on, step by step.

Doans on vacation.

I'm not going to tell you that prayer made it any easier, but somehow, we found the strength to keep going. When we crested that peak and saw the summit on the other side, a full cheer rose from our whole crew. The rest of the hike was downhill and easy.

I've never been afraid of hard work, and it's one of the key principles I've tried to instill in my children. But there are always things out of our control. We had prepared for the journey, but we didn't understand how much it would take to complete it. We gave everything we had, like always, and every one of my children remembers and tells stories about the day we hiked the

Pinnacles. At the end of that hike, we picnicked and celebrated like we'd climbed Mount Everest, all on a well-loved denim quilt that was once again a witness to our adventures.

Children and quilting alike seem to have taught me that the harder a task is, the more memorable it becomes. Don't ever let a daunting task deter you from your goals. Just take each step one piece at a time. Use your guides and follow the pattern. Stitch by stitch and step by step, don't stop until you're done. Your intentions matter, and they'll lead you to the end of your journey, wherever you want it to be. When you finish, you'll have completed something that you can be proud of.

My children have learned from Ron and me to recognize the difference between things that are worth worrying about and things that aren't. My generation was very concerned about how children looked and what they said. Children always had to be spit-and-polish presentable. With seven children following me around, I worried about all of those things. I even worried about being criticized for the number of children I had. It happened on more than one occasion, and if we didn't look put together it only increased my worries. It brings to mind another favorite phrase in our house: "Don't sweat the small stuff."

Doan family camping trip.

There is so much joy in seeing my children understand this concept even better than I did. Their generation is more able to let go of the way others perceive them and their children. They know the difference between big worries and small challenges. They'll take their children to the store in a full-on princess costume with a plastic crown and shoes. Who cares if they're wearing mismatched clothes or if they're shopping in a superhero cape? They're great at being themselves! I wish I'd realized how little people's judgments mattered. Every generation does things a little (or a lot) better than the previous one, and that self-confidence and individuality that my children have instilled in my grandchildren are wonderful qualities.

At one point, I felt like I was struggling to have enough time with each child at the end of the day. With seven children, bedtime took hours, and yet I wanted to have quality time with each of them. I tried a few different approaches, but our favorite was so simple. I would go to each child's bedside and ask them what the best part of their day was. It was a wonderful way to end the day with a happy memory.

SUMMER IN THE PARK QUILT

*S*ummer *in the Park* is a fun quilt for growing children. It's all about picnics and playing outside. Take it to your baseball games and wrap your little ones in it. Trust me, it's a quilt that will travel well! With a fun twist on a simple strip quilting pattern, this quilt will grow with the children you love as you help them create memories.

Project Info

Quilt Size
74" x 81 ³/4"

Block Size
8 ¹/4" unfinished, 7 ³/4" finished

Supply List

Quilt Top
1 roll of 2 ¹/2" print strips
1 roll of 2 ¹/2" background strips

Inner Border
³/4 yard

Outer Border and Binding
1 ³/4 yards

Backing
5 yards for vertical seam(s) or 2 ¹/2 yards of 108" wide

1 Make Strip Sets

Strip Set A. Sew a 2 ½" print strip to both sides of a 2 ½" background strip. Press the seam allowances toward the print strips. **Make 13** sets. **1A**

Strip Set B. Sew a 2 ½" background strip to both sides of a 2 ½" print strip. Press the seam allowances toward the print strip. **Make 13** sets. **1B**

2 Block Construction

Place 1 Strip Set A atop 1 Strip Set B with right sides facing. Stitch the 2 together by sewing the 2 long edges together using a ¼" seam allowance. When you have finished, you will have a tube. **Make 13** tubes. **2A**

Place a 12 ½" square ruler on a tube unit with the marked diagonal 45° center line resting on the sewn seam. Cut away the end piece and flip the ruler so the diagonal center line is on the opposite seam line. Cut 1 pieced triangle. Continue cutting the tube units in this manner. **Make 72** pieced triangles. **2B**

Press each pieced triangle block open. **2C**

Block Size: 8 ¼" unfinished, 7 ¾" finished

3 Arrange and Sew

Lay out the blocks in rows. Each row is made up of **8 blocks** across, and you need **9 rows**. Refer to the assembly diagram and turn each block in the direction indicated.

When you are happy with the layout, sew the blocks together into rows, then sew the rows together. **3A**

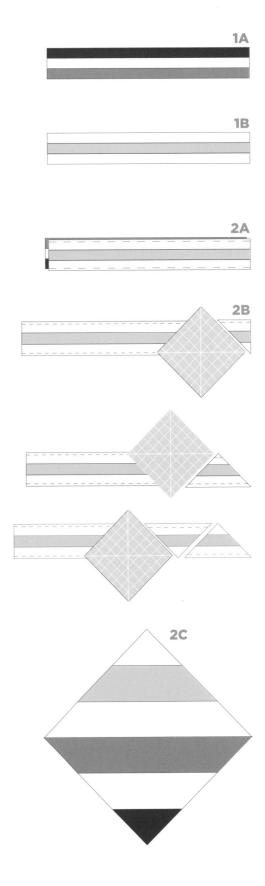

4 Inner Border

Cut (8) 2 1/2" strips across the width of the fabric. Sew the strips together end to end to make one long strip. Trim the borders from this strip.

Refer to Borders (page 181) in the Construction Basics to measure and cut the inner borders. The strips are approximately 70 1/4" for the sides and approximately 66 1/2" for the top and bottom.

5 Outer Border

Cut (8) 4 1/2" strips across the width of the fabric. Sew the strips together end to end to make one long strip. Trim the borders from this strip.

Refer to Borders (page 181) in the Construction Basics to measure and cut the outer borders. The strips are approximately 74 1/4" for the sides and approximately 74 1/2" for the top and bottom.

6 Quilt and Bind

Layer the quilt with batting and backing, then quilt. After the quilting is complete, square up the quilt and trim away all excess batting and backing. Add binding to complete the quilt. See Construction Basics (page 182) for binding instructions.

SIMPLE LOG CABIN QUILT

A *Simple Log Cabin* quilt is reminiscent of the first home a couple buys together. Using precut fabrics makes this traditional pattern even more achievable. These blocks are traditionally made with a red or yellow square in the center: red for the heart of the home or yellow for the light of the home. Both are great symbols and reminders for a marriage's start. As a couple works to start their lives together and to keep their relationship strong, even the simplest of homes can emanate love, light, hope, and peace.

Project Info

Quilt Size

63 ½" x 63 ½"

Block Size

10 ½" unfinished, 10" finished

Supply List

Quilt Top

1 roll of 2 ½" print strips

Borders

1 ½ yards

Binding

1 yard

Backing

4 ¼ yards for vertical seam(s)

Other

Scallops, Vines, and Waves Template by Quilt in a Day (available where quilting supplies are sold)

1 Sort and Cut

Choose 2 or 3 different red print strips to use as the center squares of your blocks. Cut 2 1/2" squares from the strips. Each strip will yield up to 16 squares, and a **total of 25** are needed.

Sort the remaining strips and keep 20 darks and 14 lights. Set the remaining strips aside for another project.

NOTE: If you find your package of strips doesn't contain enough light prints, you may be able to turn some prints over and substitute the wrong side of the fabric as light prints.

Keep stacks of dark and light rectangles of different lengths separate as you cut.

From each of 12 dark strips cut:
- (2) 2 1/2" x 10 1/2" rectangles
- (2) 2 1/2" x 8 1/2" rectangles

From 1 dark strip cut:
- (1) 2 1/2" x 10 1/2" rectangle
- (1) 2 1/2" x 8 1/2" rectangle

Add these to the previously cut rectangles for a **total of (25)** 2 1/2" x 10 1/2" dark rectangles and a **total of (25)** 2 1/2" x 8 1/2" dark rectangles.

From each of 6 dark strips cut:
- (4) 2 1/2" x 6 1/2" rectangles
- (3) 2 1/2" x 4 1/2" rectangles

From 1 dark strip cut:
- (1) 2 1/2" x 6 1/2" rectangle
- (7) 2 1/2" x 4 1/2" rectangles

Add these to the previously cut rectangles for a **total of (25)** 2 1/2" x 6 1/2" dark rectangles and a **total of (25)** 2 1/2" x 4 1/2" dark rectangles.

From each of 12 light strips cut:
- (2) 2 1/2" x 8 1/2" rectangles
- (2) 2 1/2" x 6 1/2" rectangles
- (2) 2 1/2" x 4 1/2" rectangles

From 1 light strip cut:
- (1) 2 ½" x 8 ½" rectangle
- (1) 2 ½" x 6 ½" rectangle
- (1) 2 ½" x 4 ½" rectangle
- (9) 2 ½" squares

Add the rectangles to the previously cut rectangles for a **total of (25)** 2 ½" x 8 ½" light rectangles, a **total of (25)** 2 ½" x 6 ½" light rectangles, and a **total of (25)** 2 ½" x 4 ½" light rectangles.

Cut the remaining light strip into (16) 2 ½" squares. Add these to the previously cut squares for a **total of (25)** 2 ½" light squares.

2 Block Construction

Using a ¼" seam allowance, sew a 2 ½" light square to the right side of a center square. Press toward the center square. **2A**

Sew a 2 ½" x 4 ½" light rectangle to the bottom of the unit. Press toward the bottom. **2B**

Sew a 2 ½" x 4 ½" dark rectangle to the left side of the unit. Press toward the left. **2C**

Sew a 2 ½" x 6 ½" dark rectangle to the top of the unit. Press toward the top. **2D**

Sew a 2 ½" x 6 ½" light rectangle to the right side of the unit. Press toward the right. **2E**

Sew a 2 ½" x 8 ½" light rectangle to the bottom of the unit. Press toward the bottom. **2F**

Sew a 2 ½" x 8 ½" dark rectangle to the left side of the unit. Press toward the left. **2G**

Sew a 2 ½" x 10 ½" dark rectangle to the top of the unit. Press toward the top to complete the log cabin block. **Make 25** blocks. **2H**

Block Size: 10 ½" unfinished, 10" finished

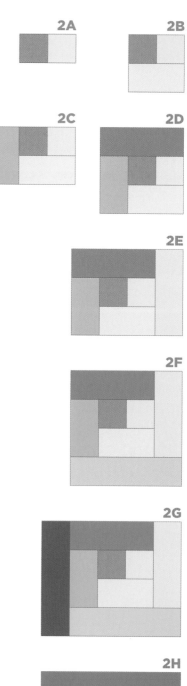

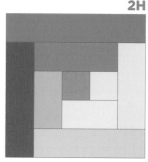

Lay out your blocks in **5 rows of 5**, paying special attention to the orientation of the blocks. Sew the blocks together in rows. Press the seams in opposite directions. Nest the seams, and sew the rows together. Press the seams toward the bottom to complete the center of the quilt top. **3A**

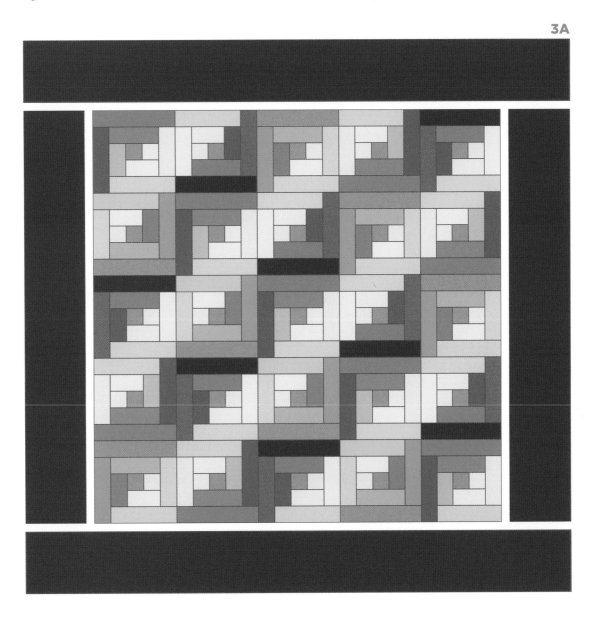

3A

4 Border

Cut (6) 8" strips across the width of the fabric. Sew the strips together end to end to make one long strip. Trim the border from this strip.

Refer to Borders (page 181) in the Construction Basics to measure, cut, and attach the borders. The strips are approximately 50 ½" for the sides and approximately 65 ½" for the top and bottom.

5 Quilt and Trim Waves

Layer the quilt with batting and backing, then quilt. After the quilting has been completed, use the Scallops, Vines, and Waves Template to mark the waves just inside the outer edge of the quilt. (Follow the instructions for measuring in the booklet that comes with the template.) Refer to the diagram on page 30 as needed and cut the wavy edges. **5A**

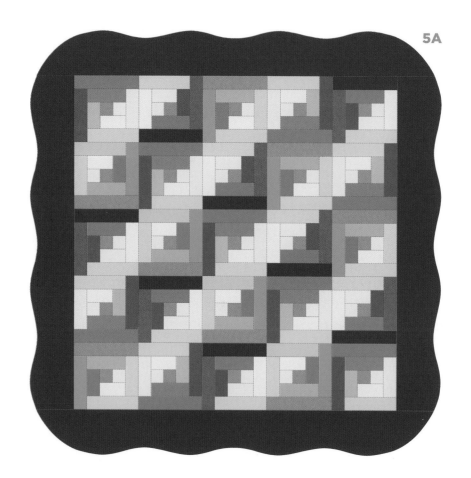

5A

6 Make Bias Binding

Because the edges of this quilt are wavy, you will need to make bias binding. From the binding fabric, cut a 30" square. Fold the square from corner to corner once on the diagonal at a 45° angle. Press a crease in place along the diagonal fold, being careful not to stretch the fabric. Place a ruler parallel to the crease and cut at least (10) 2 ½" bias strips. You'll need enough strips to total at least 285" once the strips have been sewn together. Refer to page 182 in the Construction Basics and use the Plus-Sign method to join the strips.

After the strips have been joined, gently press the strip in half with wrong sides together. Sew the binding to the front of the quilt, matching the raw edges of the binding, and quilt. Then turn the folded binding edge to the back and whipstitch in place to complete your beautiful quilt.

CHAPTER 3

SPORTS AND HOBBIES

The sounds of summer aren't complete without the hoots and hollers of a baseball game. While my kids were young, it was tradition to have at least a few family games at the local park. We waved and cheered for our teams and players while singing classic baseball songs, right up until the crack of the bat against the ball. Then the singing would turn into joyful shrieks as we jumped from our family quilt to see our team run the bases, tracking their every move.

I've spent many summer nights laughing in the grass with my family on a favorite quilt—or two, depending on how much food we brought.

Summer nights easily transitioned to fall, and the waving of brightly colored pennant flags turned into banners in Hamilton's school colors, matching minky scarves wrapped around our necks as the weather cooled. Floodlights lit the grassy field where the high school football players practiced. Soon, it was my grandchildren in cheer uniforms or carrying footballs across the field. But the laughter and cheering have never changed, and neither have the quilts. When the nights turn cold, the quilts come up off the grass, flashing their patterns and school colors as my children spectate their children's games.

We have always been a sports family, though not the official playing-on-teams variety. My kids didn't play on the community teams much. We just didn't have the money. Our family *was* the team. We had enough kids for a basketball team, and we loved to play.

Alan playing Little League.

I loved what being part of a team taught my kids: how to work together and model good sportsmanship. They learned to be kind to one another and to be aware of other people's needs.

They certainly learned that one person can't win a game by themselves. At one point, we found another family to play soccer with us. About halfway through the game, the other family was several points down and got angry because they were losing.

In true Doan fashion, my kids figured that was no big deal. Sports were important, but winning was not. "It's all good," they said. "We'll help you win."

Seth, Al, Jake, and Ron at the Richard Petty Driving Experience.

You can't imagine the looks of surprise on our friends' faces. But that spirit of competition wasn't what made us want to play! In these situations, my kids didn't want the other family to feel bad. It was about the fun of the game, and bad attitudes weren't fun. Competition is a big part of why my kids like to participate in sports—they do like to challenge themselves—but they rarely care who wins as long as it's a good game.

Turns out the other family didn't like that idea. From then on, before we ever started playing with any family, we made it very clear that we'd love to play, but it didn't matter who won. It mattered that we had a grand time.

When we managed to send a family member out onto a "real" team, the whole family supported them. It wasn't often. One year one boy would play baseball, and then the next year, someone else would want to try, and we'd all support them. I don't know how we figured it out, but if somebody really wanted to do something, we worked hard to help them accomplish it. We always supported one another. We still do.

Now that everybody has their own families, I'm watching my children run at full speed with all of their children in all manner of extracurricular activities. They have baseball and dance, one going to gymnastics, and another taking karate. They're going all over the place. I couldn't have done it.

Ron and I would gather our kids together and say, "You have to pick one thing." If it was baseball that year, Team Doan did baseball. If the majority voted for basketball, Team Doan was in for basketball. We couldn't manage everybody doing everything every season.

But oh, how things have changed. Now that my grandkids are the ones playing, we continue to spend summer evenings and fall nights losing our voices for the town Little League and high school sports teams. They still eventually have to choose, but Ron, our kids, and I have been treated to many nights of grandchild events.

When there isn't a sporting event, we gather in the fall to watch professional games. Football is a big part of our fall season. As the weather cools, we start to watch for the colors of our favorite team showing up in one another's homes and wardrobes. Jacob plants fall blooms in

Kansas City Chiefs red and gold, Sarah starts decorating her house in the team colors, and we all get excited for Red Fridays when we dress to support the team.

Sometimes we meet at someone's house, and we bring food and red-and-gold quilts. Several of the family members have quilts made in the colors of our favorite team, especially for this season. The quilts travel everywhere, keeping us warm on the bleachers of the grandkids' outdoor sporting events and wrapping our toes when we snuggle on the couch to watch a game together. That only lasts until we're all standing to shout at the television and dance around when the team does well. Football and sports in general have always been an occasion for gathering for our family. We set aside the worries of the day and cheer together for a game we can all get excited about.

Hamilton is a wonderful place for people to learn and love sports. There are huge football fans here. When the high school season starts, the whole town turns out for games, whether they have a kid playing or not. Flags wave, and we follow along as the cheerleaders chant their support of the team. Everybody contributes as we support each other. There's even a lady who brings cookies to share with the rest of the crowd.

If you happen upon Hamilton during football season, don't be surprised if the Main Street shop windows in all the stores feature more Hamilton Hornets than fabric. We've got parades and town pride like you've never experienced. One year, we sewed a huge banner to cross the main road from shop to shop. It was our way of wishing the football team well as they left to compete at the state championship.

The Doans enjoying a Royals game.

Making quilts that reflect our school spirit is so fun for me. What better way to share love and support with my kids, my grandkids, and the people they care about? Schools do us quilters a favor by starting out with high-contrast colors that make bright, eye-catching quilts. It's easy to pick a favorite pattern and some solid-colored fabric in the team colors, and within a day (or maybe two) you'll have a quilt that is the envy of every sports mom or dad in the stands.

Sports didn't end with traditional football and baseball in our family. While the kids were little, we made sure they always had access to a play area. In our backyard we built monkey bars, slides, a tetherball pole, and a low balance beam. The girls were baton twirlers for a while too—at least, until one of the rubber ends of a baton came loose midtwirl and hit Jacob in the mouth. It knocked his tooth right down his throat! He was fine, but that was coincidentally the day I took Jake to get a dog. You could say he earned it—or just paid his dues with that knocked-out tooth.

Of course, the boys had their own mishaps. Once, while practicing a baseball swing, one of them swung around and hit the sliding-glass door that spanned the back of the living room. The door did more than just break—it shattered, leaving us with nothing between the indoors and the California outdoors. That was one of the more hazardous situations our love of sports has gotten us into. If I'd been a quilter at the time, I'm sure I would have hung some fabric or a quilt top up to block the opening, but I hadn't learned that skill yet, and so it sat open. It was a good thing we happened to live in warm California, because it took us over a month to save the money to replace that door.

Any excuse to play out of doors was a good one. We loved hiking and roller skating, biking and basketball. Tetherball was a favorite game of ours. That and four square were big loves of our family. You don't see a lot of those games anymore, but in our home they came to life.

Not even car trips were safe from outdoor play. If we took a road trip, inaction only lasted as long as the drive to the next rest stop. The kids would pour from the car and run circles around the grassy areas, and before they piled back into the vehicle, I'd gather all of them together and have them make a pyramid. We'd line them all up by age and take a picture. With such an active family, it helped get some of their wiggles out until we made it to the next place.

Sports grew along with my family. Right now, the grandkids are all into disc golf and pickleball. They play together and keep track of the courses they've completed, taking discs with them

everywhere they go. No matter what it is or why someone wants to play, we'll try pretty much anything.

We even made up a few sports. It's become a tradition to play motorcycle soccer every Fourth of July. Whether we're riding or watching, everyone looks forward to the game. We gather our little collection of motorbikes and meet in the spacious backyard of my son and daughter-in-law Jake and Misty. The bikes and riders head to the grass, and the rest of us fix food, laugh, and cheer for the tiny soccer ball rocketing around the yard. It's a Doan-grown game—and, to be clear, we have found that there are reasons this game is not an official sport. We don't recommend you try it at home. It developed over time, and learning to play together has added to the fun of the holiday.

Made-up games and mashed-up fun have always fit our family well. Creatives tend to be a passionate group, and my crew easily shifted from their passion for designs, sewing, and art of all kinds to their passion for sports, throwing their hearts into their games. It is a fantastic way to divert stress, dislodge creative blocks, and just have fun.

When someone loves sports, designing a quilt really is that simple. If you make a quilt for a guy who loves football, you're not making an heirloom; you're making a quilt that is going to be used—and well. A brightly colored sports quilt will travel to games, home or away. That quilt will be thrown on the couch when he watches at home. It's going to the stadium to pad the benches or ward off the icy weather. It's going to end up flying from the back of a pickup truck or in front of the house.

Celebrating someone's love of sports is easy when it comes time to give gifts. You have a secret pass to giving them a present they'll greatly appreciate. All you have to do is find out their favorite team or sport, and voila! Just pick up half a yard of each team color and start quilting.

There aren't many gold medals or ribbons given out for quilting, and even when there are, I simply don't enjoy the competition of those events. I prefer to quilt for the joy of creating, just as my children played for fun rather than to win. People have asked me to judge quilt shows, and I always say no. Who am I to judge your creation? No quilt is perfect, and yet they all are. When you sew, you create, and you're creating exactly the quilt you need to make.

A Launchpad for Traditions

Sports have always been a creative outlet that helped my family express themselves. That expression bled into so many other hobbies. We sang, acted, read, and volunteered at the local library. With a family of amazing, homeschooled children, I did anything I could to engage their hands and minds. For a while we even participated in reenactment events, sewing period costumes to learn about American historical events.

But the most fun was when Christmas came around.

I mentioned before that our family likes to make Christmas gifts for one another. We've done this since my youngest was barely out of diapers. Frankly, we just couldn't afford to buy gifts and didn't want our kids to wake up Christmas morning with nothing to open.

In the beginning, things were a little rough. The first year we tried making gifts, nobody was certain what to do or what they were capable of. There were coupon books and baked goods, and I helped a lot! But, year by year, we got better at it, and the kids very quickly discovered the things they loved doing and making. In the end they made things like a spring-loaded ping-pong basketball game and a gumball machine formed out of mason jars and a hand-carved gumball dispenser base.

In a way, making Christmas presents for one another was its own gift. Our kids got to explore creativity and ingenuity. It was amazing to see what they came up with. Ron and I had just as much fun as the kids!

Timing was another element of our gift giving that kept this tradition especially lively. Some of the gifts were fairly intricate, taking days to complete, but they had to be kept a secret until Christmas Day. So, the kids would seclude themselves in a corner of the house, lock the door to a room, and work feverishly until their projects were ready. For us it was a necessity, but it also became a joy.

It didn't matter how much we had; the kids learned the joy of creating during those days. They put their hearts into their gifts, and that made giving them even more special. My children's creativity during those holiday adventures left them with a lot of hobbies and a willingness to try anything. Several of my children still carry on this homemade tradition in their families.

Creativity is a huge part of my family. Every one of my children is creative in one way or another. I remember when Ron began expressing his creativity and how it surprised him. He'd believed for years that he just wasn't creative, but slowly, he realized his love for hobbies and interests. Now, he bakes with the grandchildren, and he loves woodworking. He carves and whittles with our oldest granddaughter most weeks, and every Christmas the grandchildren know Grandpa is available to help make gifts for their family celebrations.

When quilting came into my life, it was simply a hobby. I already knew how to sew, but I wanted more. I had no idea the joy it would bring me and my family when I made my first little *Log Cabin* block so long ago. Simple patterns grew and changed in my mind as I switched fabrics or the direction of a block. It was like playing with life-sized kaleidoscopes. I still take time to sing, paint, act, or craft as opportunities arise, but nothing fills my bucket and my heart like quilting.

FAVORITE THINGS
QUILT

The *Favorite Things* pattern is a great place to start if you want to make a quilt for someone who loves sports. You can quickly wrap that person's favorite team or sport fabric in bold colors and just as quickly finish it to wrap them in a quilt that reflects their passion. Baseball, ballet, hockey—you name it, there's a fabric for you.

I used the *Favorite Things* quilt pattern to make Ron's football quilt. We chose the Chiefs' colors of red, gold, and black. With some fun, themed fabric in the center, I framed every block using alternating yellow, red, and black. You can do the same with your favorite team colors. When it all comes together, it looks so festive. It helps everyone to be ready for a winning game!

Project Info

Quilt Size
68″ x 77 ½″

Block Size
10″ unfinished, 9 ½″ finished

Supply List

Quilt Top
2 yards of novelty fabric
    (includes outer border)
¾ yard of red fabric
¾ yard of yellow fabric
¾ yard of black fabric
1 ½ yards of white fabric
    (includes inner border)

Binding
¾ yard

Backing
5 yards for vertical seam(s) or 2 ½ yards of 108″ wide or extra-wide 80″ Cuddle fabric

NOTES: The usable width of fabric should be at least 42″.

1 roll of 1 ½″ strips can be substituted for the white yardage.

1 Cut

From the novelty fabric, cut (13) 5" strips across the width of the fabric.
- From 5 strips, subcut (8) 5" squares.
- From 1 strip, subcut (2) 5" squares for a **total of 42** print squares.

Set the remaining 7 strips aside for the outer border.

From each of the red, yellow, and black fabrics, cut (12) 2" strips across the width of the fabric.
- From 5 strips, subcut a **total of (28)** 2" x 7" solid rectangles.
- From 7 strips, subcut a **total of (28)** 2" x 10" solid rectangles.

From the white fabric, cut (32) 1 1/2" strips across the width of the fabric.
- From 10 strips, subcut (8) 1 1/2" x 5" rectangles.
- From 1 strip, subcut (4) 1 1/2" x 5" rectangles for a **total of 84**.
- From 14 strips, subcut (6) 1 1/2" x 7" rectangles for a **total of 84**.
- Set the remaining 7 strips aside for the inner border.

2 Block Construction

Gather (1) 5" print square, (2) 1 1/2" x 5" white rectangles, (2) 1 1/2" x 7" white rectangles, (2) 2" x 7" solid rectangles, and (2) 2" x 10" solid rectangles.

Lay the (2) 1 1/2" x 5" white rectangles atop both sides of the 5" print square, right sides facing. Sew using a 1/4" seam allowance. Press. **2A**

Add the (2) 1 1/2" x 7" white rectangles to the top and bottom of the unit. Press. **2B**

Sew the (2) 2" x 7" solid rectangles to both sides of the unit. Press. **2C**

Add the (2) 2" x 10" solid rectangles to the top and bottom of the unit. Press to complete the block. **2D**

Make 14 of each color block for a **total of 42** blocks.

Block Size: 10" unfinished, 9 1/2" finished

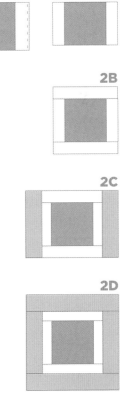

2A

2B

2C

2D

3 Arrange and Sew

Arrange the blocks in **7 rows of 6**. Notice how the block colors alternate across the rows. Once you are happy with your arrangement, sew the blocks together to form a row. Press seams in opposite directions. Nest the seams, and sew the rows together. Press to complete the center of the quilt top. **3A**

4 Inner Border

Gather the (7) 1 1/2″ strips set aside for the inner border. Sew the strips together to make one long strip. Trim the borders from this strip.

Refer to Borders (page 181) in the Construction Basics to measure, cut, and attach the borders. The strip lengths are approximately 67″ for the sides and 60 1/2″ for the top and bottom.

5 Outer Border

Gather the (7) 5″ strips set aside for the outer border. Sew the strips together to make one long strip. Trim the borders from this strip.

Refer to Borders (page 181) in the Construction Basics to measure, cut, and attach the borders. The strip lengths are approximately 69″ for the sides and 68 1/2″ for the top and bottom.

6 Quilt and Bind

Layer the quilt with batting and backing, then quilt. After the quilting is complete, square up the quilt and trim away all excess batting and backing. Add binding to complete the quilt. See Construction Basics (page 182) for binding instructions.

RIBBON STAR QUILT

The *Ribbon Star* reminded me of the prizes we give to celebrate our sports players and crafters when they've done really well. It's great to have a pattern that's easy, quick, and rewarding, and the *Ribbon Star* is just that. You can tailor your ribbon colors to your favorite teams.

Project Info

Quilt Size
68″ x 82″

Block Size
12 1/2″ unfinished, 12″ finished

Supply List

Quilt Top
1 roll of 2 1/2″ print strips
1 roll of 2 1/2″ background strips
1/4 yard of background fabric

Outer Border
1 1/2 yards

Binding
3/4 yard

Backing
5 yards

NOTE: If you wish, you can substitute 3 yards of background fabric and cut a **total of (42)** 2 1/2″ strips across the width of fabric.

1 Cut

Select (20) 2 ½" x 42" print strips. From each, cut (4) 2 ½" x 6 ½" rectangles. Keep each set of four together.

Select (20) 2 ½" x 42" print strips. From each, cut (4) 2 ½" x 4 ½" rectangles. Keep each set of four together.

From the leftover pieces of the 2 ½" print strips, select 20. From each, cut (4) 2 ½" squares. Keep each set of four together.

From the remaining pieces of the 2 ½" print strips, cut (30) 2 ½" squares for sashing cornerstones. Set aside.

From the background fabric, cut:
- (240) 2 ½" squares
- (80) 2 ½" x 4 ½" rectangles
- (49) 2 ½" x 12 ½" rectangles. Set aside for sashing.

2 Make Corner Units

Sew a 2 ½" background square to a 2 ½" print square. Add a 2 ½" x 4 ½" background strip as shown. **2A**

Sew a 4 ½" print strip to one side of the unit as shown. Add a 6 ½" print strip to the adjacent side. **2B**

Fold (2) 2 ½" background squares from corner to corner once on the diagonal, and press the crease in place. Using the crease as your sewing line, stitch a square to each of the two print strips of the unit as shown. Trim the excess fabric ¼" away from the seam line. **Make 4** for each block. **2C**

Sew the 4 corner units together to complete the block. **Make 20** blocks. **2D**

Block Size: 12 ½" unfinished, 12" finished

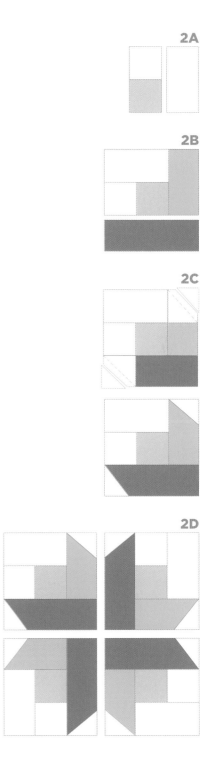

2A

2B

2C

2D

3 Arrange and Sew

Lay out the blocks in rows, with each row containing **4 blocks**. Once you are happy with the appearance, sew the blocks together into rows, adding a 2 1/2" x 12 1/2" sashing rectangle between each block and on the two outside edges. **Make 5** rows. **3A**

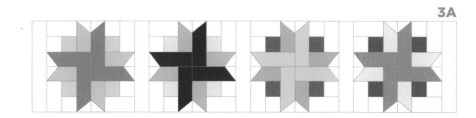

3A

4 Sashing Strips

Sew a 2 1/2" square (cornerstone) to a 2 1/2" x 12 1/2" sashing rectangle. Add a 2 1/2" square, then another sashing rectangle. Continue on in this manner until you have sewn a strip containing 5 cornerstones and 4 sashing rectangles. **Make 6** sashing strips. **4A**

Sew a sashing strip between each row of blocks. Finish the center of the quilt by sewing one sashing strip to the top of the quilt and one to the bottom.

4A

5 Border

From the border fabric, cut (7) 5 1/2" strips across the width of the fabric. Sew the strips end to end to make one long strip. Sew the strips together. Trim the borders from this strip.

Refer to Borders (page 181) in the Construction Basics to measure and cut the inner borders. The strips are approximately 72 1/2" for the sides and approximately 68 1/2" for the top and bottom. **5A**

6 Quilt and Bind

Layer the quilt with batting and backing, then quilt. After the quilting is complete, square up the quilt and trim away all excess batting and backing. Add binding to complete the quilt. See Construction Basics (page 182) for binding instructions.

CHAPTER 4

GRADUATION

The next stop on our quilted journey of life is graduation! Whether it's from high school, college, trade school, the military, or another institution, graduating is something worth celebrating. It's my tradition to make graduation quilts for my grandchildren. I can't tell you how much I treasure this opportunity. It's a special chance to show them how much they mean to me. The best part is watching them get excited over this gift from their grandma. And you better believe every one of them has taken those quilts with them as they've traipsed off to college or other adventures.

Oftentimes, graduation is celebrated at a commencement ceremony after the conclusion of years of learning. The graduates have completed something grand, so we post the bold colors of their alma maters, bring out the choirs and prestigious alumni, and make lists of the greatest achievements among the group. It's a lot of fanfare to celebrate the end of something when it is really the beginning of a new part of life—the beginning of where the real learning takes place.

I've always loved to learn. Finding out how things work, practicing a new skill, discovering a new pattern—it all brings me so much joy. I never want to stop learning. It's part of me and my creativity.

When I was younger, people didn't always understand my unique inquisitiveness. I liked to know why I was expected to do things or why a certain principle or formula would get the answer teachers wanted from me. But "Why?" was not a question that was appreciated in those days.

I didn't know it then, but my determination to learn everything challenged the way people thought. I remember walking into the counselor's office once to say, "I'm not getting algebra."

His answer? "Take business math. You'll never use algebra because you're a girl."

I was having a hard time with the concepts, and his solution was to take an easier class. Even at that age, I was stunned!

Years later, I worked at a school for boys and sat in on another algebra class. The way this teacher explained it, I picked it up right away. *That's all it is?* I said to myself. All I needed was clarification and explanation. That counselor had the ability to shape my future, but due to society's expectations, I didn't get the opportunity to learn because I was a girl.

I can assure you, I don't let expectations stop me often. I wore shorts under my dresses so I could play on the monkey bars, since at that time girls weren't allowed to wear pants to school. I was the first girl in my high school to take a woodshop class, and I ran those machines right alongside the boys. I didn't understand why a boy would be allowed to do something but a girl wouldn't. It was unfair.

Even my creativity got me in trouble. When I wanted to take a calligraphy class, the instructor told me I couldn't because I was left-handed. Apparently, left-handed people can't write calligraphy because our hands cover the words as we write and smear the ink.

Not only was I a girl, but I was a left-handed girl.

If I could insert an eye roll here, I would. I am not afraid of hard work. When someone tells me I can't do something, it's as bad as being told a pattern can't be done a certain way. If there is a way, I'll figure it out. With that in mind, it won't come as a surprise to you that I didn't let them tell me I couldn't learn calligraphy. I was confident I could.

"I want to take calligraphy," I told the teacher. "I know I can do this, and I'm going to take this class." And that was that.

I had to learn to write sideways and backward to keep from running my hand through the ink, but I did it. I made my own pens and designed my own lettering.

I fought for those opportunities. I've always been a fighter, a rule breaker. That fighting spirit has brought about some of the most memorable moments in my education, not always because of what I learned but because of the strength it took to learn it.

Similar challenges faced me as I brought my ideas into the quilting world. I didn't know how things had always been done, or should be done, so I did things my way. No one told me there were rules, so I didn't follow them. When I looked at a quilt block or pattern and questioned why it was made like that, no one jumped out to stop me. By trying new things, I found shortcuts that surprised and delighted quilters around the world.

A few people questioned if my version of quilting was as good. If I didn't make blocks the same way they had always been made, would it hurt the final product? Those questions quickly disappeared as we broke down barriers to quilting that people didn't even know existed.

I came at this craft from a different angle. People who had always thought they couldn't quilt because it was too hard saw how I was sewing and realized they could do it too. We learned together that there are no Quilt Police. It was a freedom of creativity that got quilters new and old excited!

I love seeing people find strength and passion in learning new methods. As part of a homeschooling family, my children have had the freedom to learn what they wanted to learn. And it's taken them further than we expected. As they reached graduation age, it was hard for me to send them out into the world, mostly because I would miss them. But just as I watched them grow and stretch beyond the reach of their baby blankets, watching them grow into themselves and seek out life and adventure beyond school was empowering.

Homeschooling isn't for everyone, but it was the best option for us, and I loved it. English was one of my favorite subjects. The kids wrote every day. They got to where they wrote such hilarious things, they could hardly wait to read their stories to one another. I would start them off with a prompt like, "I was walking along a country road, and suddenly . . ." and off they'd go.

I never knew what they'd come up with. I heard everything from "a spaceship landed" to "a lawnmower came around the corner." We laughed so hard at those funny stories!

The ability to learn is an integral part of human life, and I wanted our children to find and cherish the joy it held. I don't have cookie-cutter children. Regardless of the direction they chose moving into the next phase of their lives, they've all reached markers of accomplishment. It was important to Ron and me that we made each of their achievements a point of celebration.

That has continued with my grandchildren, and making quilts to celebrate their graduations has blossomed into an exciting tradition. We spend time together, planning and collaborating on their quilts. Sometimes I have an idea of what I want to make for them, and other times I let them pick out the pattern and colors. It's a fun memory we have together, and remembering what went into the quilt helps them feel comforted when they are away from home. As I cut, stitch, and iron, it helps me feel closer to them as well.

I have one granddaughter who loves cats. She is all fun and games. When I found a full cat-themed panel in her favorite colors, I couldn't resist.

One of my grandsons, who'd been working with us in the filming studio at the time, has a great eye for design. He picked one of my patterns and then redesigned it to be unique to him. I loved helping him create his own vision.

When my oldest granddaughter graduated, I made her quilt with a special message sewn into the pattern—one she could look at and hold close and be reminded how valuable she is. She picked the fabrics and colors, but I made it for her in secret. It was all wonky stars. Each was different, and each was beautiful. I wanted her to know that we don't have to be perfect to be valuable. We all shine in our own space with our own light. It was a quilted message I wanted her to carry as she went out into the world.

Noah and Jenny and his graduation quilt.

As young adults graduate, it's so important to celebrate them. The way we honor them helps them know they're valued by us. A quilt is such a beautiful way to acknowledge their efforts, echoing their education in longevity and detail. Both the quilt and education will stay with them through the years. It becomes an heirloom of accomplishment that they'll treasure forever.

One of my younger granddaughters was unable to decide on just one pattern and asked if she could get one quilt when she graduated high school and another when she graduated from college. Of course, I said, "Yes! Graduation is always an accomplishment!"

Sometimes things get in the way of our celebrations, and important moments don't look the same as we expected. One year I had two granddaughters graduating high school, and I was gearing up to get both quilts done when our little town received heart-wrenching news. Two of their friends and classmates had unexpectedly passed away. Everyone's hearts broke, and no one felt like celebrating. As phone calls and loving gatherings circulated, the terrible losses touched all members of the community. The graduation of my granddaughters' high school class—the same ceremony those two students who'd lost their lives would have participated in—was only weeks away, and all anyone wanted to do was cry, wrap their arms around one another, and cry again.

I would have put my arms around every child and teacher in that school if I could have. So, I did the only thing I knew how to do. I sewed quilts. Natalie, Sarah, and I made quilts in a rainbow of colors. There were sixty students in the graduating class, and losing two of them left a noticeable hole in every heart. We made a quilt for every graduating student. No matter where they were or what they were doing, they could wrap up in those quilts and feel individually loved. It was another quilted message.

Jenny with granddaughter Annie wrapped in a quilt.

As a quilter, one of the most poignant ways we have to share our love is making a quilt. The receiver may not know what goes into it, but we do, and that's our gift to give. We spend so much work and time trying to convey love. That work is our way to honor them and their accomplishments. To me, that's important. It's a piece of our heart that goes with them and transcends time as they mature and move through the phases of life. All we can do is hope it makes them feel cared for, secure in themselves, and that they believe they're worthy of this gift.

WONKY STARS
QUILT

*W*onky Stars **is the quilt** I made for my oldest granddaughter's graduation. It's a simple and incredibly versatile quilt. The hardest part is letting yourself be really free with sewing nontraditional angles. Once you get comfortable with that, you're all set. Every block should end up different, and using scraps can help that process along. The resulting stars will carry messages of love, joy, beauty, and individuality, all personal to you and your loved one.

Project Info

Quilt Size
69" x 82 1/2"

Block Size
14" unfinished, 13 1/2" finished

Supply List

Quilt Top
1 package of 10" print squares that has duplicate prints
1 package of 10" background squares

Inner Border
3/4 yard

Outer Border
1 1/2 yards

Binding
3/4 yard

Backing
5 yards for vertical seam(s) or 2 3/4 yards of 108" wide

1 Cut and Group

Cut each 10″ square in half vertically and horizontally to make (4) 5″ squares. Stack all matching squares together. If the package of 10″ squares you are using does not have duplicate prints, use squares that have the same color value.

Group together (13) 5″ squares for each block. Use 5 print squares and 8 background squares to **make 10 blocks**. The remaining 10 blocks use 8 print squares and 5 background squares.

2 Make Print Star Points

Select (2) 5″ squares, 1 print and 1 background. Fold the background square in half and finger-press a crease at the midway point along the bottom edge. Place the print square atop the background square with right sides facing at an angle. The print square should overlap the marked halfway point. Sew the print square in place using a ¼″ seam allowance. Trim ¼″ away from the sewn seam. **2A**

Press the piece flat, turn the square over, and trim all edges evenly with the background square. **2B**

Place the trimmed print scrap on the adjacent side of the square with right sides facing at an angle. Make sure the edge of the scrap crosses over the first print by at least ¼″ and will cover the corner when trimmed. Sew in place using a ¼″ seam allowance. Trim the excess fabric away ¼″ from the sewn seam. **2C**

Press the print piece over the seam allowance. Turn the square over and trim so all edges are even. Notice the square is still 5″. **Make 4** units. **2D**

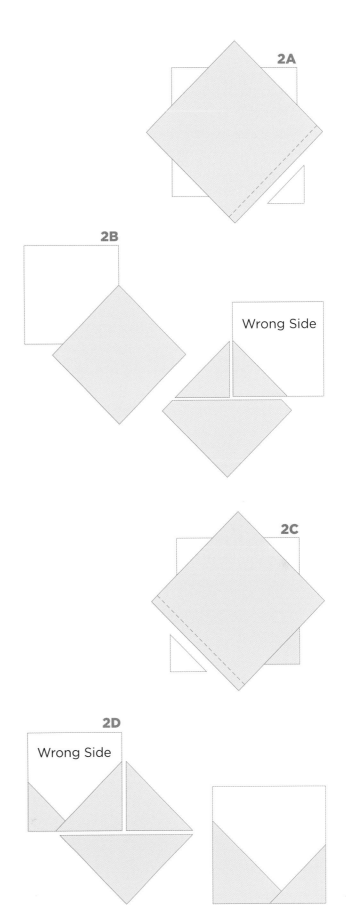

3 Block Construction

Sew a 5″ background square to either side of a star point unit. **Make 2** rows in this manner. **3A**

Sew a star point to either side of a 5″ print square. **Make 1** row in this manner. **3B**

Sew the 3 rows together to complete one block. **Make 10** blocks. **3C**

Block Size: 14″ unfinished, 13 ½″ finished

3A

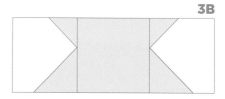

3B

4 Background Stars

Follow the directions for the print stars but trade fabric placement. Where previously a background square was used, use a print square instead and vice versa. **Make 10** units. **4A**

Block Size: 14″ unfinished, 13 ½″ finished

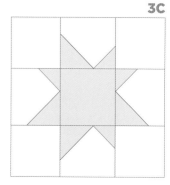

3C

5 Arrange and Sew

Lay out the blocks in **rows of 4**, alternating a print star with a background star. **Make 5** rows. Press seams in opposite directions. Nest the seams and sew the rows together. Press to complete the center of the quilt top. **5A**

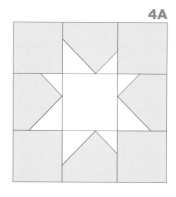

4A

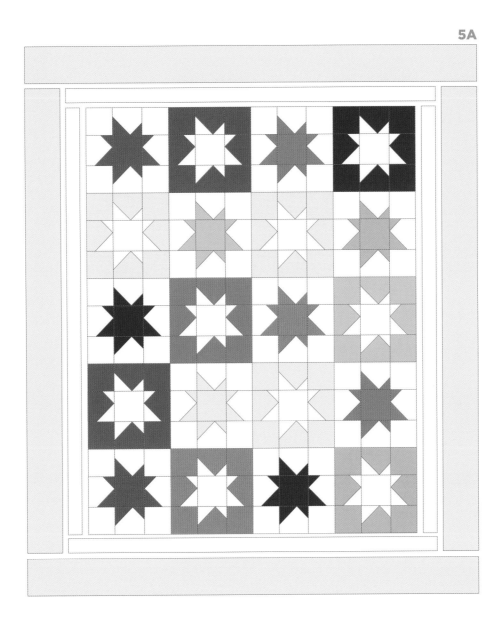

6 Inner Border

Cut (7) 2 ½" strips across the width of the fabric. Sew the strips together end to end to make one long strip. Trim the borders from this strip.

Refer to Borders (page 181) in the Construction Basics to measure and cut the inner borders. The strips are approximately 68" for the sides and approximately 58 ½" for the top and bottom.

7 Outer Border

Cut (8) 6" strips across the width of the fabric. Sew the strips together end to end to make one long strip. Trim the borders from this strip.

Refer to Borders (page 181) in the Construction Basics to measure and cut the outer borders. The strips are approximately 72" for the sides and approximately 69 ½" for the top and bottom.

8 Quilt and Bind

Layer the quilt with batting and backing, then quilt. After the quilting is complete, square up the quilt and trim away all excess batting and backing. Add binding to complete the quilt. See Construction Basics (page 182) for binding instructions.

PINWHEELS ON POINT
QUILT

*S*trips and half-square triangles are combined to make this sensational quilt. The beautiful border made from trimmed scraps adds another dimension. You can highlight the pinwheels by piecing them in the graduate's school or favorite colors to make it even more special. With a quilt full of pinwheels waving, it will feel like they get to keep celebrating their achievements.

Project Info

Quilt Size
58" x 74"

Block Size
16 ½" unfinished, 16" finished

Supply List

Quilt Top
(1) 2 ½" roll of print strips—
    includes outer border
1 yard of white fabric
1 yard of solid fabric

Inner Border
½ yard

Binding
¾ yard

Backing
3 ¾ yards for horizontal seam(s)

1 Make Strip Sets

Sew 4 contrasting strips together. Press all the seams in the same direction. Cut each strip set into 8 ½″ squares. Trim carefully; you may need to allow a bit of selvage in the seam allowance to get the required number of squares from a strip. **Make 48** fence rail blocks. **1A**

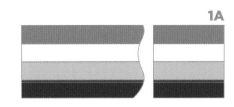

2 Cut

From the white fabric, cut (3) 10″ strips across the width of fabric. Subcut the strips into 10″ squares for a **total of 12** squares.

From the solid fabric, cut (3) 10″ strips across the width of fabric. Subcut the strips into 10″ squares for a **total of 12** squares.

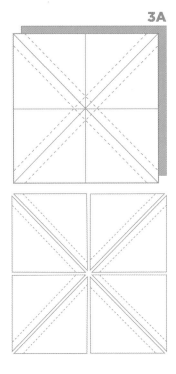

3 Sew

On the reverse side of the white square, draw a line from corner to corner twice on the diagonal. Place the white square atop the solid square and sew ¼″ away from either side of the drawn lines. Cut straight through the center of the squares horizontally and vertically with your rotary cutter, then cut along the drawn lines. You will have 8 half-square triangles. **Make 96** half-square triangles. **3A**

Open each and press the seam toward the darkest fabric. Trim the half-square triangles to 4 ½″. **3B**

Fold and press a crease into the half-square triangle going across the seam line. **3C**

Place a half-square triangle on the lower right corner of the fence rail block with right sides facing. Stitch in place by sewing on the crease. Sew another seam toward the outer edge ½″ from the stitching line. **3D**

Repeat for the upper left corner. The colors of the half-square triangles should be opposite of the first corner. This will form the pinwheel in the middle of the large block. **3E**

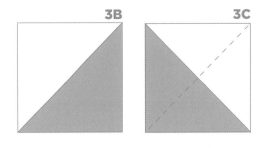

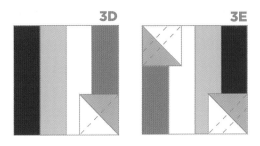

Using a rotary cutter, slice between the two sewn seam lines, leaving ¼" on either side of the cut. Open and press the corners of the block flat. Reserve the trimmed units for the border. **3F**

Sew 4 rail fence blocks together to make one large block. Each block should be turned until a pinwheel forms in the center. **Make 12** blocks. **3G**

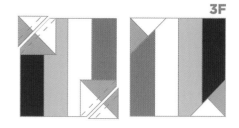

4 Arrange and Sew

Arrange the blocks into **4 rows of 3**. Once you are happy with your arrangement, sew the blocks together to form a row. Press seams in opposite directions. Nest the seams, and sew the rows together. Press to complete the center of the quilt.

5 Inner Border

From the inner border fabric cut (6) 2 ½" strips across the width of the fabric. Sew the strips together end to end to make one long strip.

Refer to Borders (page 181) in the Construction Basics to measure and cut the inner borders. The strips are approximately 64 ½" for the sides and approximately 52 ½" for the top and bottom.

6 Outer Border

Open and press the trimmed units that were set aside when making the blocks. Square each to 3 ½". **6A**

Measure the quilt through the center vertically. Sew enough 3 ½" units to equal that measurement (approximately 68 ½"). A strip of 23 will be a bit too long. Adjust the length by using a larger seam allowance in several places. **Make 2** and sew one to both sides of the quilt.

Measure the quilt through the center from side to side, including the borders. Sew enough 3 ½" units to equal that measurement (approximately 58 ½"). Nineteen blocks will be a bit short, so use a scant ¼" seam allowance when sewing the pieces together. **Make 2** and sew one to the top and one to the bottom of the quilt. **6B**

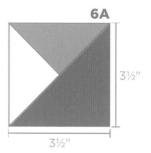

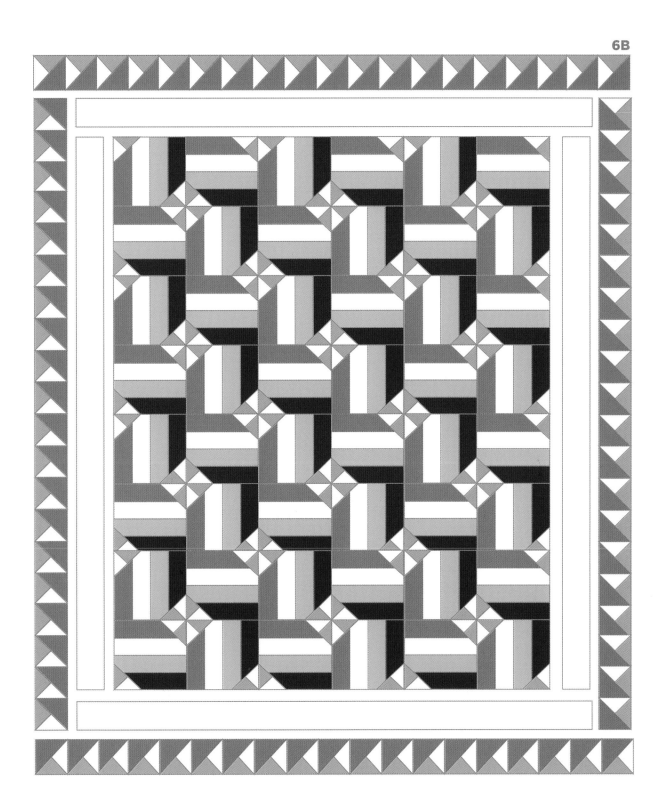

7 Quilt and Bind

Layer the quilt with batting and backing, then quilt. After the quilting is complete, square up the quilt and trim away all excess batting and backing. Add binding to complete the quilt. See Construction Basics (page 182) for binding instructions.

CHAPTER 5

MARRIAGE

Ah, the wedding quilt.

Can you hear the sighs?

The idea of the wedding quilt came from an era when women brought full dowries into a marriage. Trunks of handmade linens, napkins, pillowcases, and all things needed to start a home were carefully crafted and curated from the time a young lady was born.

One of the last items that went into the trunk was the wedding quilt. After painstakingly sewing intricate patterns and designs in order to impress your prospective spouse with your homemaking skills, it took the efforts of a community to hand-quilt and bind it together. The wedding quilt was the crowning jewel of the dowry. A couple's first quilt for their first bed together.

Ahem. Well, I think it's safe to say that times and traditions are changing. Beds are bigger than ever, and styles of bedding range from simple quilted sheets of fabric to intensely colored patterns or fluffy creations impossible

Al and Drea's wedding day with Doan Family members.

to fit under a home sewing machine. Even the thought of trying to fulfill all the particular expectations with all those choices has my heart racing—and not with romance! Trying to piece together perfection for the happy couple translates into an insane amount of pressure.

I remember asking one of my daughters what she wanted for her wedding quilt. The conversation went something like this:

"What size should I make it?"

"King-sized!" Or maybe it was a California King. I don't remember, though I clearly recall how her smile grew and mine tightened at the thought of the huge quilt.

After swallowing that information, I asked what style she'd like.

"I was thinking it would be good to be something a little different but timeless. Kind of a cross of styles. Something modern but also traditional . . . -ish."

My expression must have spoken for me, because she quickly shared that she had collected an online gallery of some of her favorite patterns. "I already started because I knew you'd offer to make our quilt," she assured me. "You can pick the one you want to make most. I just don't want it to be too stressful or challenging for you."

How sweet . . . and kind of insulting? I just kept smiling and tried to take it as a kind consideration as she pulled up her collection of inspiration pictures. All of the quilts were completely different styles, and her modern-traditional mishmash of quilts was no help in figuring out what I should make.

"And for colors, you know my favorite . . . But I want to keep it muted. Probably . . . unless you want to do a bright quilt. I totally trust your judgment, of course . . ."

I love her, but at the end of the day, she had no idea what she wanted. No one ever told me I had to read minds to make a wedding gift.

Unfortunately, I've had versions of this experience over and over again. I put so much time, energy, and emotion into making a marriage quilt, and I soon realized how impossible it was to make each couple's vision come true. Most of them had a hard time even settling on colors, much less patterns and designs.

We forgive them, of course; their brains are tainted with romance, wedding plans, and wedding stress. It's a lot of pressure to put on both a new couple and a quilter.

The imagery of the wedding quilt is full of beauty and unrealistic expectations. But tradition is very clear: when a couple gets married, you make them a quilt. Right? Well, maybe.

Today, it no longer requires an entire community to make a quilt for a lace-packed trousseau. Newly engaged couples shop and register for bedding in a wide range of styles and budgets to create a beautiful bedroom set. Even when

Ron and Jenny with Misty and Jake on their wedding day.

someone decides on the perfect colors or patterns, it will likely change as quickly as the sales at their favorite home décor store. And that is 100 percent okay. I change the quilt on my own bed every four or five months.

So, what does this mean for a generous and kindhearted quilter who only wants to make a young couple's dreams of their first quilt come true?

It means you're off the hook.

A quilt made for someone you love—for any reason—is an incredible treasure, and as a wedding gift, it will always be remembered. You can still make a quilt for the newlyweds if your ambition is telling you to. I chose a different route.

A few years ago, I decided to unburden myself of the expectation of making wedding quilts. I no longer make bedding.

Now, I make picnic quilts.

Picnic quilts are smaller than the massive king- or queen-sized bed quilts requested by so many newlyweds. They can be any size and any color. And they serve a great purpose: to encourage the couple to keep dating, even beyond the wedding. That's some of the best advice I've been able to give to my grandchildren, nieces, and nephews as they have gotten married. I always include a note with their quilt that says, "I want this to be used and loved." Then I place the quilt in a basket with some picnic supplies, and I have an instant wedding gift that's fun and personal.

By calling it a picnic quilt, I give them permission to use it, to make it their car quilt. I want them to toss it on the grass, or on the sand, and snuggle with it under the stars. It will be the keeper of their memories. These picnic quilts carry a little piece of my heart and are quite possibly the most genius change I've made to my gifting habits in years.

A Wedding Quilt for Jenny and Ron

I wasn't a quilter when Ron and I met. When we fell in love, it took me by surprise. I'd been married before for a short while, and I wasn't used to experiencing love the way I did with Ron. I'm grateful for that every day.

Our wedding was casual, sweet, and exactly what I wanted. I'd been making my own clothes for years, but making a wedding dress was a scary prospect. Still, I knew what I wanted, and my close friend's mother helped me make it a reality. The dress didn't have any extra fluff or frills. White satin shaped the fitted bodice and the floor-length A-line skirt. The shoulders were draped with a capelet I'd designed. It hung to my elbows in the front and well below my waist in the back. Instead of a veil, I wore a delicate ring of wildflowers and baby's breath. I made matching flower crowns for Natalie as the flower girl and my brand-new baby, Sarah. I still have her tiny ringlet of dried flowers on my wall.

Ron wore a gray plaid suit and the biggest smile I'd ever seen. He held my heart in his hands as I walked down the aisle to meet him. Our reception was at my mother's house in California—an old Victorian with a beautiful backyard filled with flowers and brick walkways. I loved the whole thing.

A simple wedding for a simple love and a simple life. It was all I wanted.

For our wedding, I made Ron a jean quilt. I didn't finish it until a little after our wedding,

Jenny and Ron feeding each other cake on their wedding day.

but I'd been busy with a baby and wedding plans, and Ron didn't mind. I wanted to give him a gift I'd made with my own hands. A sturdy quilt for picnics, adventures, and memories. I sewed all those jean squares together and backed the whole thing in train fabric. He loved trains. Back then, I was quilting without knowing it—I was just sewing squares together—and yet it was exactly what we needed.

I didn't want another pretty decoration. I wanted something to *live* with!

When Ron and I got married, we promised to love each other unconditionally. We've done our best to hold true to that promise. Hurt feelings still happen, but simple miscommunications are usually to blame. In any marriage, regular, positive, clear communication is key.

Good, decent relationships look easy, though they never are. Every marriage is hard in its own way. Everybody has disagreements. Marital problems aren't solved through wishing. It takes hard work. As in quilting, there is no magic needle and thread to repair mishaps. If something is miscut, you try again, fix your mistakes, or reread the instructions to see where you went wrong. The benefit (and challenge) of a relationship is that you're working with a partner. The quilt the two of you are making is meant to be shared. As you recognize your partner's talents and skills, you'll find ways to make the finished product more than it would be with your work alone.

Have you heard the adage "You love the people you serve"? It's an original life hack. As a natural doer, it resonates deeply with me that service and love are tightly connected. *Love* is an action word, after all. So, when my darling husband irritates me—because that happens, even to us—I do nice things for him. I write kind notes to put in his lunch, make his favorite meal, take time to iron his shirts, or plan a date that I know he'll enjoy. Early in our marriage I found the

things he appreciated, and my heart changed as I showed him my love through simple service. As a bonus, he came home kinder, sweeter, and feeling more appreciated.

Regardless of the problems I wished Ron would fix, when I put a note in my husband's lunch that said, "You have the most gorgeous eyes I've ever seen. Have a great day!" it reminded us both that we're important to each other.

As the years progress, these expressions of kindness and love can begin to feel commonplace, falling away as life wraps us up tighter and tighter. But that doesn't diminish the difference they make when we take the time to make someone feel cared for. Of course, some problems are bigger than notes in your partner's lunch. But when you love others the way you expect to be loved, those simple acts of kindness can change the feeling in your home and relationship.

The trick here is that you can't change somebody else; you can only change yourself. You are serving your partner. It takes effort to keep bringing your kindest, best self to the person you love the most in the world. It's a game of giving and receiving, but when you both play, it will teach you how good it feels to be intentionally loved.

X'S AND O'S
QUILT

The *X's and O's* quilt is an instant win for a wedding picnic quilt. It represents love without being all hearts and flowers. I used to get cards from my grandma, and at the end it would have an *x* and an *o* or several *x*'s and *o*'s. As I was learning to read, I thought she had added a word I didn't understand into my special note.

One day, I asked my mom, "What does qua qua qua (*xo xo xo*) spell?"

She laughed when she saw Grandma's message. "It's a hug and a kiss!"

I loved that, and I love having that secret note stitched into a quilt. With only a few packs of 5″ squares and a little bit of background fabric, this quilt full of hugs and kisses is perfect for newlyweds. You can smile every time you connect another *X* and *O*, spelling out a secret message of encouragement to keep up the romance, as your loved ones take their new quilt on many adventures.

Project Info

Quilt Size
68″ x 77″

Block Size
9 ½″ unfinished, 9″ finished

Supply List

Quilt Top
4 packages of 5″ print squares
2 packages of 5″ white squares

Inner Border
¾ yard

Outer Border
1 ½ yards

Binding
¾ yard

Backing
4 ¾ yards for vertical seam(s) or 2 ½ yards of 108″ wide

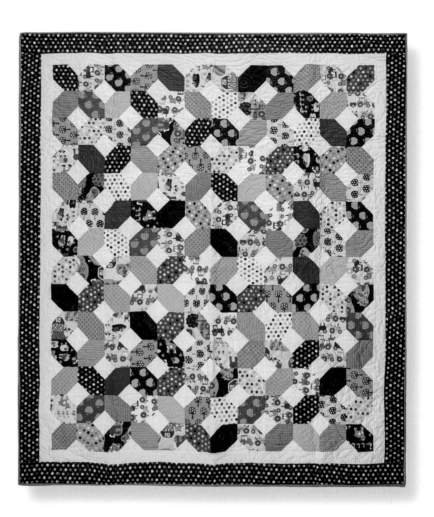

1 Cut

Cut (84) 5″ white squares in half vertically and horizontally for a **total of (336)** 2 ½″ squares. **1A**

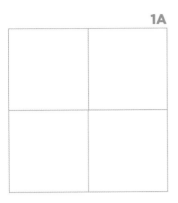

2 Sew

Fold each 2 ½″ white square once on the diagonal and press. Sew a square to two opposing corners of a 5″ print square, using the crease as the stitching line. **2A**

Trim the excess fabric ¼″ away from the seam line. **Make 168** block units. **2B**

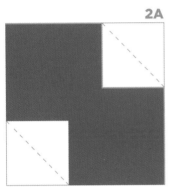

3 Block Construction

Stitch 4 units together as shown to make one block. **Make 42** blocks. **3A**

Block Size: 9 ½″ unfinished, 9″ finished

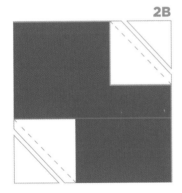

4 Arrange and Sew

Sew **6 blocks** together to make a row. **Make 7** rows. Press seams in opposite directions. Nest the seams and sew the rows together, then press to complete the quilt center. **4A**

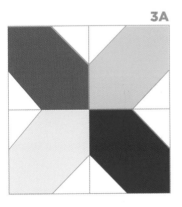

5 Inner Border

From the inner border fabric, cut (7) 2 1/2" strips across the width of the fabric. Sew the strips together end to end to make one long strip.

Refer to Borders in the Construction Basics (page 181) to measure and cut the borders. The strips are approximately 63 1/2" for the side borders and 58 1/2" for the top and bottom.

6 Outer Border

Cut (8) 5 1/2" strips across the width of the fabric chosen for the border. Sew the strips together end to end to make one long strip.

Refer to Borders in the Construction Basics (page 181) to measure and cut the outer borders. The strips are approximately 67 1/2" for the side borders and 68 1/2" for the top and bottom.

7 Quilt and Bind

Layer the quilt with backing and batting, then quilt. After the quilting is complete, square up the quilt and trim the excess backing and batting away. Add binding to complete the quilt. See Construction Basics (page 182) for binding instructions.

OPPOSITES ATTRACT QUILT

*O*pposites Attract **is made from** a star quilt block that is split down the middle with a starkly contrasting fabric on either side. Black and white. Lavender and green. Red and cream. You pick what works for you, because the colors don't matter as much as the contrast.

In marriage we often choose people who are very different from ourselves. That's not a bad thing, though it may require us to work harder at the small things our partner may not recognize we need. Don't be afraid of the differences; celebrate them by finding what you love about your significant other. Find the aspects in each other that are both contrasting and complementary in your relationship.

The *Opposites Attract* quilt only exists because of the differences in either side of the quilt block. Both fabrics are different. But when the whole pattern comes together, it's the contrast that makes it beautiful.

Project Info

Quilt Size
59" x 69"

Block Size
8 ½" unfinished, 8" finished

Supply List

Quilt Top
1 package of 10" print squares
1 ½ yards of sashing fabric
    (includes inner and middle
    borders)

Outer Border
1 yard

Binding
¾ yard

Backing
3 ¾ yards for horizontal seam(s)

Other
Clearly Perfect Slotted Trimmer A (recommended)

1 Sort and Cut

Sort the 10″ print squares into 20 pairs of light and dark. Set the remaining squares aside for another project.

NOTE: Each pair of squares will make 1 block. It is important to keep all of these pairs together once they are cut to make block assembly easier.

From each of the 10″ print squares:
- Align 1 pair and cut them in half both vertically and horizontally to make (4) 5″ square pairs. **1A**
- Set 2 pairs of 5″ squares aside for half-square triangles.
- Cut the remaining (2) 5″ square pairs in half vertically to make (4) 2 ½″ x 5″ rectangle pairs. **1B**
- Subcut 2 rectangle pairs into (4) 2 ½″ square pairs. **1C**
- Trim 1 rectangle pair to 2 ½″ x 4 ½″. **1D**

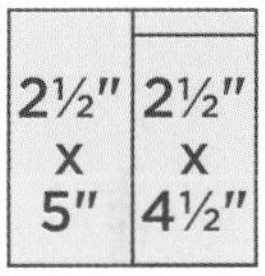

Set aside 2 pairs of the 2 ½″ squares and the 2 ½″ x 5″ rectangle pair for the sashing and scrappy border.

From the sashing fabric:
- Cut (8) 2 ½″ strips across the width of fabric.
- Subcut a **total of (31)** 2 ½″ x 8 ½″ rectangles for sashing. **1E**
- Set the remainder of the sashing fabric aside for the inner and middle borders.

1A

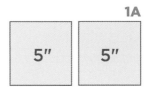

1B

1C

1D

1E

2½″ x 8½″	2½″ x 8½″	2½″ x 8½″	2½″ x 8½″	
2½″ x 8½″	2½″ x 8½″	2½″ x 8½″	2½″ x 8½″	
2½″ x 8½″	2½″ x 8½″	2½″ x 8½″	2½″ x 8½″	
2½″ x 8½″	2½″ x 8½″	2½″ x 8½″	2½″ x 8½″	
2½″ x 8½″	2½″ x 8½″	2½″ x 8½″	2½″ x 8½″	
2½″ x 8½″	2½″ x 8½″	2½″ x 8½″	2½″ x 8½″	
2½″ x 8½″	2½″ x 8½″	2½″ x 8½″	2½″ x 8½″	
2½″ x 8½″	2½″ x 8½″	2½″ x 8½″		

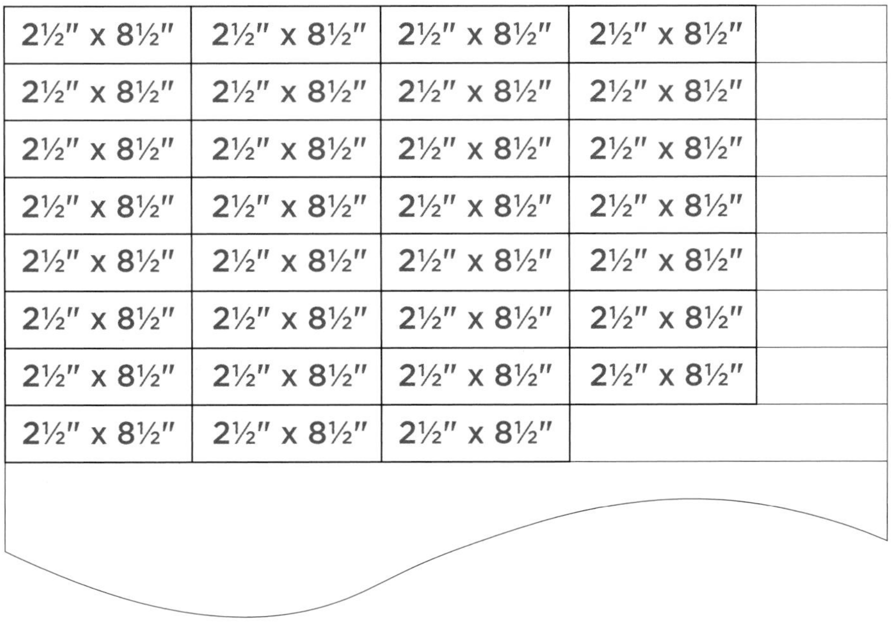

2 Make Half-Square Triangles

2A

Select 1 set of light and dark print units. Place the 5″ light square atop the 5″ dark square, right sides facing. Sew around the perimeter. **Make 2** units. **2A**

2B

Cut the sewn squares twice diagonally. Use the Clearly Perfect Slotted Trimmer A to trim the half-square triangles to 2 ½″, then press open. Each set of sewn squares will yield 4 half-square triangles for a **total of 8** half-square triangles. **2B**

NOTE: If you are not using the slotted trimmer, press your squares open first and then square to 2 ½″.

3 Block Construction

3A

Place the 2 ½″ x 4 ½″ light rectangle atop the dark rectangle, right sides facing. Sew along the long edge and press. **3A**

3B

Pair the half-square triangles as shown to create 1 dark point, 1 light point, and 2 mixed points. Notice that the 2 mixed points must have light and dark fabric in opposite positions. **Make 4** star point units. **3B**

Arrange the units just made, along with (2) 2 ½″ light print squares and (2) 2 ½″ dark print squares from your set, into rows as shown. Pay close attention to the placement of the light and dark fabrics. **3C**

Sew the units together in rows and press in opposite directions.

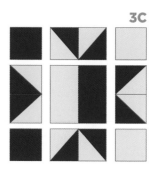

3C

> **TIP:** Press the seams of the center row inward and press the top and bottom rows outward.

Nest the seams and sew the rows together. Press. **Make 20** blocks. **3D 3E**

Block Size: 8 ½″ unfinished, 8″ finished

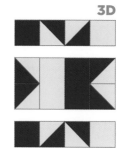

3D

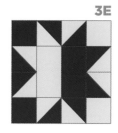

3E

4 Make Sashing Strips

Gather 12 of the 2 ½" print squares set aside earlier along with (16) 2 ½" x 8 ½" sashing strips. Arrange (4) 2 ½" x 8 ½" sashing strips with (3) 2 ½" squares, as shown. Sew to form a row and press. **Make 4** horizontal sashing strips. **4A**

4A

5 Arrange and Sew

Lay out the blocks in **5 rows of 4** with a 2 ½" x 8 ½" sashing rectangle in between each of the blocks. **5A**

5A

NOTE: Each block has the dark side on the same side throughout the quilt.

Sew the blocks and the 2 1/2" x 8 1/2" sashing rectangles together to form rows. Press. Sew the rows together with the horizontal sashing strips, then press to complete the quilt top.

6 Inner Border

Cut (10) 2 1/2" strips across the width of the sashing fabric. Sew the strips together to make a long strip. Trim the borders from this strip.

Refer to Borders (page 181) in the Construction Basics to measure, cut, and attach the borders. The strip lengths are approximately 48 1/2" for the sides and 42 1/2" for the top and bottom. Set the remainder of the long strip aside for the middle border.

7 Pieced Border

Gather all of the leftover 2 1/2" squares and 2 1/2" x 5" rectangles set aside earlier. Sew the pieces together, alternating between squares and rectangles, to make a long strip. Trim the borders from this scrappy strip in the same manner as before. The strip lengths are approximately 52 1/2" for the sides and 46 1/2" for the top and bottom.

8 Middle Border

Gather the long strip of sashing fabric set aside earlier. Trim the borders from this strip in the same manner as before. The strip lengths are approximately 56 1/2" for the sides and 50 1/2" for the top and bottom.

9 Outer Border

Cut (6) 5" strips across the width of the outer border fabric. Sew the strips together to make a long strip. Trim the borders from this strip.

Refer to Borders (page 181) in the Construction Basics to measure, cut, and attach the borders. The strip lengths are approximately 60 1/2" for the sides and 59 1/2" for the top and bottom.

10 Quilt and Bind

Layer the quilt with backing and batting, then quilt. After the quilting is complete, square up the quilt and trim the excess backing and batting away. Add binding to complete the quilt. See Construction Basics (page 182) for binding instructions.

CHAPTER 6

NEW STARTS

With all its new beginnings, springtime holds a special kind of joy. The season breaks free from the cold, bringing flowers to life and sprouting fresh leaves and green grass in its place. There's so much color and life. The beauty of spring taught me early on that starting again isn't something to be afraid of. New beginnings happen all the time.

When my kids were little, one of my favorite things to do was go around to their rooms at bedtime and talk with them. I'd ask them about their day and their favorite thing that happened. It was always so sweet to hear what they enjoyed, but sometimes they'd tell me things hadn't gone so great. Those days, I'd pull them close, snuggle them, and remind them that tomorrow was a new beginning, and they'd get to start over and try again.

When every day is new, life isn't a race or a competition. It's about trying again and inching forward moment by moment. And we don't have to throw out the old to start again. A fresh start can be anything you put new or renewed effort into. It's not just a beginning, it's a *new* beginning.

Every milestone we pass in life is a kind of new beginning. Graduation, marriage, or having babies—are all familiar changes we experience and even anticipate. What about moving into a new home or learning a new skill? These new starts make an impact on a person's life, leaving an emotional imprint that we often discount. Like fabric scraps, swept off the table after trimming a quilt block, we don't usually give them a second thought. But there could be a whole quilt under your sewing table if you take the time to stitch together the scraps worth saving.

When Ron and I were first married and had moved into our first home together, it was exciting—and a little scary. I'd been away from home before, but this was different. I felt like my life was finally moving in the right direction. We were a brand-new family moving into the tiny place we'd rented that was just big enough for us and our girls. It wasn't in the greatest part of town, and it didn't really feel like home, but I was really good at making things work.

As we unpacked and tried to settle in, I came across a specific shelf that I'd had in my room since high school. I knew just where I wanted to hang it. I nailed it in place and set my blue plates up for display, and a funny thing happened. Suddenly this little house in its questionable neighborhood became *home*.

Items and memories can change our perception, and making that space mine gave my heart ownership.

It's a funny thing, but it never fails: we hang a certain decoration or put out a specific piece of furniture, and suddenly we belong in that space with our things. It becomes part of our traditions, part of our heritage. Our children remember those things, and their children remember. They become part of us.

That feeling of home can be achieved in lots of ways. Now, when I move into a new space, I choose several dedicated "quilt walls" and quickly hang my quilt display rods. As the quilts go up, they line the walls in warmth and make the whole space friendlier. It's as if the quilts give us a hug and welcome us in.

The first quilt Jenny made was a *Log Cabin* quilt.

If I were to take one of those quilt walls and put a picture there instead, it wouldn't have near the meaning. I can't help but get excited when I pull out a quilt to hang and Ron says something like, "Oh, I love that one." It's high praise to know your work is being loved by people you love.

Wherever I live, I've always had a porch on my home; it's sort of a requirement for me. When we moved to Missouri, we bought a home with a large, wraparound porch that I love for a lot of reasons. One of the biggest reasons is that I get to hang porch quilts, and they brighten the whole neighborhood. The vibrant designs float like a banner proclaiming, "I love quilts!" and "You are welcome here!" Quilts can be vocal like that—inviting people in.

Quilts are a joy in my life and sharing them in such a public way had a contagious effect; they started popping up around town! Whenever I see a quilt flying from a porch ceiling, happiness weaves its way around my heart. It's a connection to our community that lifts me up and makes neighbors friends as we share our communal love of quilts.

My family didn't move often. We started out in California, renting instead of purchasing a home. The ability to own a house was a distant dream. But eventually, it happened. Welcoming my family into that first little pink house was a moment of such gratitude for me. Even with the pink bathtub, deep red-speckled carpet in the dining room, and gold shag in the living room, I was thrilled that it was ours. No, it wasn't pretty from a design perspective, but it was gorgeous to me. We had moved into a new stage of our lives with nothing but our belongings and children in hand.

We didn't move again until we decided to pack up and take our expanding family to the middle of the country. Moving to Missouri was one of the biggest adventures of our lives, with more unknowns than I can count. We didn't have a clear picture of where we were going at all, just that it was time to move. We had a lead on a place to stay and a job lined up for Ron, so we left the only home our marriage had ever owned. We both left family behind us in California, including our oldest son, who stayed for college. We said goodbye to friends, play groups, craft groups, walking trails, the ocean, familiar grocery stores, the banks we liked, the knowledge of what to do with free afternoons, and all our comfortable surroundings—so many little things we hadn't considered when we sold off our excess belongings in a garage sale and drove halfway across the country.

There were lots of reasons not to go, but what we found when we moved to our new town changed our lives forever. We found a community that was safe and carefree. We left doors unlocked and spent evenings outside talking with neighbors. We found fields to run in and friends to love. We found a world that fit my soul.

No one could tell me and my family what to expect as we began this new adventure in rural Missouri. Change was the only thing I could depend on. So I opened a door in my heart and invited whatever was waiting on the other side to come inside. It was as terrifying as it was hopeful, but the gamble was worth it, through and through. With the rich culture of quilting in this area, and the people around us, each piece helped our future fall into place. Quilts made a world of difference in easing that change, wrapping uneasy emotions in love, sharing excitement and fears.

Creativity Under Constraint

Quilters have to be particularly good at new beginnings. Every change of the season and new event calls for a new pattern or project. Sometimes we're so good at this that our lives become overrun with unfinished quilts we've begun and then set aside, waiting for the inspiration and desire to complete one. So we press forward, setting our sights on new projects, bringing them into the vacated space of old ones, and hoping this time we'll find the motivation to finish. The whole process is a flourishing example of new beginnings. In quilting and life, there's always room for a fresh start.

Quilting as a whole was a new beginning for me. I knew nothing about the craft; I sewed clothing and costumes. I didn't know what a *four-patch* (a block of four squares) was or understand the significance of lights and darks in the pattern instructions. References to *WOF* (width of fabric) went right over my head as I read my first patterns, and I laughed and barked out a playful "woof" back at the paper. It was an entirely new language—and more so, a new world.

I'd had a bit of exposure to quilting from family and friends and even attended a one-night course where I spent my time following directions but mostly chatting with friends. It took me almost another full year before I sought out my first real class. I found one in a neighboring town where they had a vocational tech college with classes on everything from welding to auto mechanics—and, yes, quilting. Some friends had told me about the class, and I decided to reach out to the teacher. When I signed up, quilting was foreign and overwhelming to me. So, I convinced the teacher to go shopping with me, and we drove forty minutes away to Macon and the nearest quilt shop. She helped me pick out four light fabrics and four dark fabrics while I asked a lot of questions. Then I went home and waited for the class to begin.

Once a week I spent an hour with that teacher and a room full of women, learning this new skill. I can't tell you how much I looked forward to it. Wednesday evenings became my sanity night. These days, classes and instructors are available online at any given moment. But at that point in my life, I waited eagerly for that special night every week. Then, seven days later, I packed up my supplies and drove thirty minutes away to do it again.

It was a fresh start, packed into a classroom of quilters.

Those Wednesday nights saved me. One night a week may not seem like much, but look closer. I had children in school from elementary to college. Some were getting married, others going to college and leaving the nest. Any time to myself was difficult, and to give myself a night off to go take a class was next to impossible.

More of my friends were moving on, moving out, and moving away. I was personally drained. For so many years, everything I'd had to give went to my family: my creative endeavors, my heart, my time, my love. I was focused on being a mother and wife first. I don't regret that choice, but I had forgotten how to be me. All I had left were emotional endings. What else could I do? I needed a new start for me, for my life.

That's what quilting did for me. I took one night a week and gave myself something to look forward to. I'd go out and do something I loved. After several months, the class ended, but I continued to sew with some of those ladies every week. I didn't know it at the time, but taking that class didn't just change my schedule; it changed me. It refueled my heart and my creative reservoirs. I found a new passion and learned a new skill . . . and from that moment on I never stopped.

I truly believe that learning keeps our creative juices flowing. Knowledge feeds creativity. Even now, if I'm feeling drained, I take a class on something I know nothing about, and I'm rejuvenated again. I've taken a marble class, a pottery class, even a beekeeping class! I'll try whatever's available as long as it piques my interest and creativity. I love how learning feels. I crave that growth.

A few years ago, my son Alan asked me when I'd felt the most *successful.* It took me back a bit. Success is not something I've ever placed as a goal. Growing up, success meant getting my own place, having a job, owning my own car. I accomplished most of those things by the time I was eighteen. If Al could have asked about my life then, I would have told him my success felt complete, like I couldn't go any further. But there was more to come.

As I look back at how much I've accomplished since setting out on the beginnings of my adult life, the answer to his question wasn't one of the obvious moments of accomplishment, and it surprised us both.

"You know," I told him, "I think it was the day I went to the grocery store and checked out without first thinking about a food plan."

"Your success was buying food?" He didn't seem to believe me.

"Sort of." I laughed. "It was more about the budget. Never in my life had I not had to worry about how many pennies I have left in my bank account. So that moment in the store—buying food without first calculating the cost—was success for me. It was freedom."

Living in California, our expenses were (understandably) high. For more than twenty years, my job had been feeding my family of nine people on a zipper-tight budget. After our bills, I usually had around fifty dollars to spend on food. I went to the grocery store with four lists— you can imagine them as tiers. I had my list of dinner foods that we needed, a separate list of things I wanted to get, another of things I hoped I would get, and finally a list of miracle foods or items. (I called them miracle foods because it would have been miraculous if we were able to purchase them.) Needs, wants, hopes, and miracles. We rarely reached the fourth list at all, but with coupons and careful planning, I'd always managed to feed my family.

The day I could go to the store and comfortably choose my purchases from each list was a kind of success that I couldn't have known I would feel so deeply.

There is no blueprint for success, and there shouldn't be. It isn't dictated by what we accomplish but by how we feel about what we accomplish. The list of things we do to reach that feeling will change and adapt as much as we do. So, I try to look at success differently. The way I see it, we either choose when we've made it, or we'll feel like we never really get there at all. It's a beautiful thing that we can let ourselves feel successful every day of our journey.

Success for me was about being able to take care of and have the necessities. It has never mattered to me that I had the newest car; it mattered that I had a car. It didn't matter that I had a perfect house; it mattered that I had a place to live. And any place I lived, it mattered to me that I left it better than it was before.

When we didn't have much, each week became a game of creative successes, and I got very creative. As did my children. Creativity thrives under constraint. I believe those habits led us to some great places. We were never afraid to try something new.

That ingenuity and willingness to try quite likely led to one of the biggest new beginnings in my life: starting a business. I can promise you that was never part of any of my to-do lists. In fact, I'm not much of a businesswoman at all.

A baby quilt Jenny made for her granddaughter Hannah. See *Breezy Windmills* on page 8 to make this quilt.

I'm an idea girl. I love coming up with new, fun ways to do something. People sometimes comment on the success of our company, but I'm as much in awe as anyone. I didn't do any of it alone. None of us could. I had my family helping me and making things happen. They all have different strengths that make this business work, which has come with its own set of challenges.

The best part of running a business with my family is that I get to spend every day with my children. And the worst part of it is that I get to spend every day with my children. But believe me when I tell you the best part is so much better than the worst. I love that our relationships have stayed close and that we have a common goal. That's also a hard part—because sometimes quilting is really all we do, and when you know everything someone is doing, it makes for fairly monotone conversations.

When our company started out, I was promoted from regular mom to company mom. I took care of everyone who worked with us, ensured that things went smoothly, and invested in

Jenny's doll quilt.

every aspect of the business. There's an amazing gift that comes from doing this. I learned how valuable every employee in the company was, from the customer service agents in the back office to the fabric cutters and shop clerks. I also quickly realized that it's impossible to do it all myself—even though I tried. I battled my son at one point not to spend more money hiring a cleaner "because I could do it." I reasoned that I could work harder, come in earlier, stay later, whatever was needed. A cleaner seemed like an excess expense to me at the time. It took Alan pointing out that the money spent to hire a cleaner would make the work I was doing easier to finally change my mind. I couldn't do it all, and nobody was asking me to.

That was a hard lesson. I had to let go of my mothering instincts and home in on what I did well so that those working with us had the opportunity to do the same.

Maybe you can do it all, but you shouldn't. You have to find your magic. I was doing what I loved, and it was time to let go and let the rest of the people around me find their magic. If you don't love creating but you're really good at handling social media, there is a place for you. Maybe you don't love working in the storefront, but if you're great with solving problems, your magic is needed, and there is a place for you. We work hard to find our employees' magic because if they love what they do, they'll do it well. And when everybody loves what they're doing, things run as smoothly and happily as an automated quilt machine, dancing through a pattern without missing a stitch.

This new adventure was at the same time the most wonderful and most nerve-wracking thing

I'd ever done—or tried to do. It was exciting at first, and then it got really scary. We came across certain things I knew I couldn't handle, and my only choice was to hope my kids and employees were smart enough to know what I didn't.

Our business had an unfathomably good start. It's grown so much—and keeps growing thanks to the amazing people who work with us, support us, and learn with us. Every customer is a new beginning. They invite us into their homes, tell us their story, and carve out space in their lives for what we have to offer.

Quilting affects people in largely different ways, but it always changes them. They come to this craft thinking they're just sewing, and before they know it this progression sweeps them up. I meet people who tell me they've healed emotional and physical wounds through quilting. Others may tell me they got through a divorce because of quilting. Or that quilting helped them grieve a lost loved one.

We're better people because of the work and art we share. To create something is to heal. We don't often realize at first that this will happen, but across the board, it does happen.

It's an amazing gift, and it's all because we made a new start.

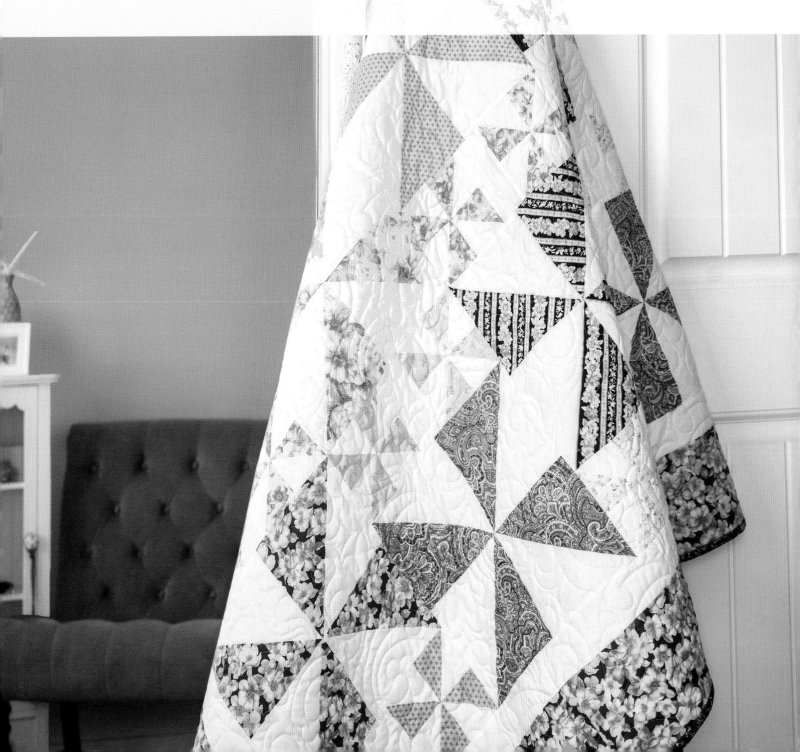

PINWHEEL PICNIC
QUILT

The *Pinwheel Picnic* is a simple starter quilt that helps you succeed no matter your skill level. Find a fabric you love, and use this new pattern to make some magic as you start a new project.

Project Info

Quilt Size
83" x 87"

Block Size
17 ½" x 12 ½" unfinished,
    17" x 12" finished

Supply List

Quilt Top
1 package of 10" print squares
1 package of 10" background
    squares
1 yard of background fabric
    (includes inner border)

Outer Border
1 ½ yards

Binding
¾ yard

Backing
8 yards for vertical seam(s) or 2 ¾ yards of 108" wide

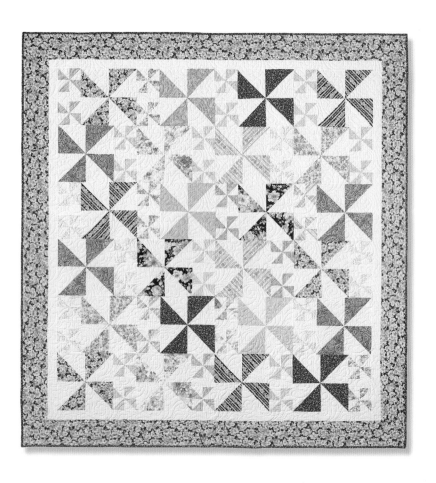

1 Cut

From the background yardage, cut (12) 2 ½″ strips across the width of the fabric. Subcut 4 strips into 2 ½″ x 5 ½″ rectangles. Each strip will yield 7 rectangles. A **total of 24** rectangles are needed.

Set aside the remainder of the strips for the inner border.

2 Large Half-Square Triangles

Select (24) 10″ print squares. Layer each with a 10″ background square with right sides facing. Sew all around the perimeter of the layered squares using a ¼″ seam allowance. Cut the sewn squares from corner to corner twice on the diagonal. Open each section to reveal a half-square triangle unit. Press the seam allowance toward the darker fabric and square each to 6 ½″. **2A**

Sew 4 half-square triangles together as shown to make a pinwheel. **Make 24** pinwheels. Set aside for the moment. **2B**

3 Small Half-Square Triangles

Select (12) 10″ print squares and (12) 10″ background squares. Cut each square into (4) 5″ squares.

Layer a 5″ print square with a 5″ background square with right sides facing. Sew all around the perimeter of the layered squares using a ¼″ seam allowance. Cut the sewn squares from corner to corner twice on the diagonal. Open each section to reveal a half-square triangle unit. Press the seam allowance toward the darker fabric and square each to 3″. **2A**

Sew 4 half-square triangles together as shown to make a pinwheel. **Make 48** pinwheels. Set aside for the moment. **2B**

4 Block Construction

Sew a small pinwheel to either side of a 2 ½″ x 5 ½″ background rectangle. **4A**

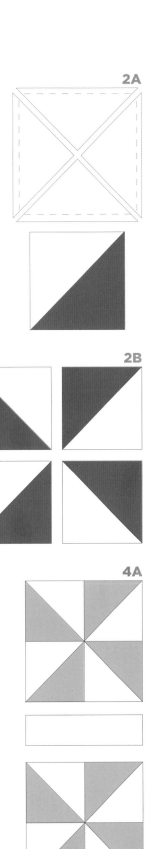

Sew a large pinwheel to the side of the sewn small pinwheels to complete the block. **Make 24** blocks. **4B**

Block Size: 17 ½" x 12 ½" unfinished, 17" x 12" finished

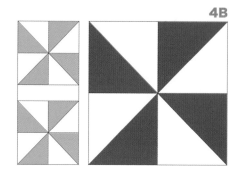

5 Arrange and Sew

Lay out the blocks in rows. Each row is made up of **4 blocks** across, and **6 rows** are needed. Sew the blocks together into rows. **Make 3** rows that begin with the small pinwheels on the left. **Make 3** rows that begin with the large pinwheel on the left. Refer to the diagram if necessary. Sew the rows together to complete the center of the quilt. **5A**

6 Inner Border

Pick up the (8) 2 1/2" background strips you put aside earlier. Sew the strips together end to end to make one long strip. Trim the borders from this strip.

Refer to Borders (page 181) in the Construction Basics to measure and cut the inner borders. The strips are approximately 72 1/2" for the sides and approximately 72 1/2" for the top and bottom.

7 Outer Border

Cut (8) 6" strips across the width of the fabric. Sew the strips together end to end to make one long strip. Trim the borders from this strip.

Refer to Borders (page 181) in the Construction Basics to measure and cut the outer borders. The strips are approximately 76 1/2" for the sides and approximately 83 1/2" for the top and bottom.

8 Quilt and Bind

Layer the quilt with backing and batting, then quilt. After the quilting is complete, square up the quilt and trim the excess backing and batting away. Add binding to complete the quilt. See Construction Basics (page 182) for binding instructions.

PRAIRIE FLOWER
QUILT

he *Prairie Flower* quilt is a pattern that won't make you wait to carry it with you on all your adventures. Drag it along and throw it in the car or wrap up with it. This is for your new start. Prairie flowers grow in a vast, fairly empty expanse. Solitary blooms where it may have seemed empty. Whether you're feeling drained or you're looking to create that blank slate so you can move forward on a new start, this is your quilt.

Project Info

Quilt Size

74" x 89 ½"

Block Size

14" unfinished, 13 ½" finished

Supply List

Quilt Top

1 package of 10" print squares
3 ½ yards of background
    fabric (includes sashing
    and inner border)
¼ yard of cornerstone fabric

Outer Border

1 ½ yards

Binding

¾ yard

Backing

5 ½ yards for vertical seam(s)
    or 2 ¾ yards of 108" wide

1 Cut

From each 10" print square, cut (4) 5" squares for a **total of 160** squares.

From the background fabric cut:
- (20) 2 ½" strips across the width of fabric. Subcut the strips into 2 ½" squares for a **total of 320** squares.
- (3) 5" strips across the width of the fabric. Subcut the strips into 5" squares for a **total of 20** squares.
- (11) 2 ½" strips across the width of the fabric. Subcut the strips into 14" x 2 ½" rectangles for a **total of 31** sashing rectangles.

From the cornerstone fabric, cut (1) 2 ½" strip across the width of fabric. Subcut the strip into 2 ½" squares for a **total of 12** squares.

2 Block Construction

Fold a 2 ½" background square from corner to corner on the diagonal and press the crease in place. The crease marks your sewing line. Fold (16) 2 ½" background squares. **2A**

Sew a 2 ½" background square onto 2 opposite corners of a 5" print square. Trim each ¼" away from the seam line. These units go on the corners of the block. **Make 4** corner units. Set aside for the moment. **2B**

Sew (2) 2 ½" background squares to 2 corners of a 5" print square as shown. The squares are on adjacent corners. These units go between the corner units. **Make 4** center units. **2C**

3 Sew Rows

Sew a corner unit to both sides of a center unit as shown. **Make 2** rows. **3A**

Sew a center unit to both sides of a 5" print square. **Make 1** row. **3B**

Sew the three rows together to make one block. **Make 20** blocks. **3C**

Block Size: 14" unfinished, 13 ½" finished

2A

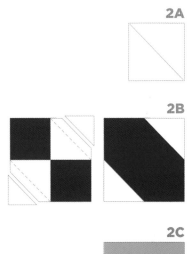

2B

2C

3A

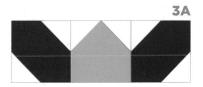

3B

3C

4 Arrange and Sew

Lay out the blocks in rows with each row containing **4 blocks**. Once you are happy with the appearance, sew the blocks together into rows, adding a 2 ½" x 14" sashing rectangle between each. **Make 5** rows. Press the seams toward the blocks. **4A**

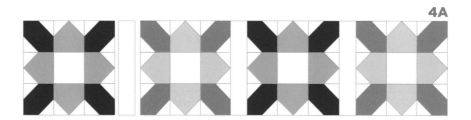

4A

5 Sashing Strips

Sew a 2 ½" cornerstone square to a 2 ½" x 14" sashing rectangle. Add another 2 ½" cornerstone square, then another sashing rectangle. Continue on in this manner until you have sewn a strip containing 3 cornerstones and 4 sashing rectangles. **Make 4** sashing strips. **5A**

   Sew a sashing strip between each row of blocks.

5A

6 Inner Border

From the background fabric cut (8) 2 ½" strips across the width of the fabric. Sew the strips together end to end to make one long strip. Trim the borders from this strip. **6A**

   Refer to Borders (page 181) in the Construction Basics to measure and cut the inner borders. The strips are approximately 76" for the sides and approximately 64 ½" for the top and bottom.

7 Outer Border

From the outer border fabric cut (8) 5 ½" strips across the width of the fabric. Sew the strips together end to end to make one long strip. Trim the borders from this strip.

Refer to Borders (page 181) in the Construction Basics to measure and cut the outer borders. The strips are approximately 80" for the sides and approximately 74 ½" for the top and bottom.

8 Quilt and Bind

Layer the quilt with batting and backing, then quilt. After the quilting is complete, square up the quilt and trim away all excess batting and backing. Add binding to complete the quilt. See Construction Basics (page 182) for binding instructions.

CHAPTER 7

LOSS AND GRIEF

At some point in our quilting journeys, we were each a beginner. Maybe you're at the beginning now, or maybe you started years ago, but you probably know as well as I do the confusion of reading a pattern for the first time. Then there's the absolute awe of the designs we struggle to create. Quilt making is an exciting and frustrating addiction.

As a new quilter, I would sit down to sew, pulling fabrics and my shaky knowledge together, and inevitably I'd mess it up somehow. I'd get a piece flipped around, sew a block set together backward, or miscut entire stacks of fabric pieces. My thread would jam, my sewing machine would eat the fabric, my bobbin would empty itself without so much as a warning, and all of my work would be rendered seemingly unusable.

I've botched many projects with my own mistakes and inexperience. Some are small errors, fixable in thirty seconds or less by ripping out a misplaced seam and redoing the stitches. Other mistakes are bigger, such as miscutting the last pieces of fabric from my grandmother's dress. No loss is too small to be comforted, and I like to believe anything can be made over to your benefit. But all mistakes are not made equal, and some just aren't as fixable.

Loss and grief walk hand in hand like sisters, trailing ragged footprints behind them. The world around us shifts when we cross paths with those sisters. The patterns change. We change. Loss is both simple, complex, and unforgiving all at the same time. Grief happens, more often than not, when loss is irreversible.

When my children were young, Natalie had a bright-blue pet parakeet that we kept in the living room in a tall cage. It was a funny little bird that played with the kids and tried to talk to us. Every time I vacuumed, she'd flap around and grip the top of the cage with her feet, hanging upside down as I cleaned. When I got to her cage, I'd tip it to the side and vacuum underneath while she swung from the cage ceiling.

Natalie had a friend visit one day. This girl believed all things should be free. Shortly after her visit we learned she'd set our little parakeet free in the backyard. We never saw it again.

Natalie was heartbroken, and so were the rest of us. I'd gotten used to the chatter of birdsong, and we missed the silly antics. She left a hole in our hearts.

I've always loved animals, and I've had a lot of them in my life. My dad usually brought animals home from business trips or traveling. Our first family pet was a little dog named Fiddie that Dad rescued. I was in elementary school when he brought me a chipmunk that liked to play in my yo-yo bedspread. Then came a horned toad in a shoebox and a little bird named Alice from Alisal.

No matter how we tried to take care of those animals, they didn't last long in our home. Fiddie couldn't adjust to having people around; he loved us but not so much our visitors. It broke my heart when he bit the neighbor boy and we had to take him back.

The chipmunk was discovered by our cat and received a scratch that got infected. The toad ran away, leaving behind the lovely box home and guaranteed food we'd provided for him. The bird—well, in trying to save little Alice's life, she passed away.

But our hardest loss came as an adult with a beautiful dog named Sadie.

We had gotten Sadie as a young rescue dog. She lived with us from our time in California all the way through our cross-country move to Missouri. Roaming all over the farm where we lived, chasing cars, and keeping watch over our home and family, she loved the change as much as we did. Her sudden death was a shock to us all. While chasing a truck, Sadie was hit by the back wheel of a trailer.

She was just a farm dog, I told myself. *These things happen.* I'd never been torn up by the loss of a pet . . . My heart didn't care how many times I made excuses. We'd lost a member of the family when Sadie died.

Grief blocked my willingness to understand what had happened, and it took our children's insistence on getting a new dog before I was able to bring another animal into my life. Children can be a blessing in these circumstances.

Jenny with one of the family dogs.

When adults lose a pet, we often feel, *I can't love another animal*, so we don't even try. But if your kids are like mine, they're fairly insistent that you get another pet after a loss. Maybe not right away, but it always feels like they'll be bringing one home if we don't do it first.

The blessing is that with a pet, often what you really need is companionship—a reason to get up every day and keep going. Children help you through the rough patches by creating that pressure to move forward, and soon you find your heart opening again.

Every day after, loss forces you forward. Even when you're hurting, you get up. You keep going. When a quilt block made of treasured fabric is lost, the entire project isn't heaped unfinished in the corner. What a waste that would be! Instead, you fill in the gaps with whatever you can find. You finish because the project as a whole is important. The pattern changes, and the rest of the quilt shifts around the lost piece. Even though it's not what it was before, it's still beautiful.

No one lives untouched by loss. It's as simple as a child moving away from a best friend or as big as a family member dying unexpectedly. I've experienced the loss of homes, jobs, stability, family older than me, family younger than me. They don't hurt the same every time, but they all hurt. A loss is a loss.

There are phases of pain and grief when you lose something or someone in your life. Everyone's journey and understanding are different, and you can only help in relation to what you know. I have to remind myself that, in times of loss, I can only help from where I am.

At one time, I had a good friend whose son took his own life. This loss resonated through the community, but as much as I cared about her, I could only do so much. As a supporter several circles outside of her and her family, I can remember feeling helpless because I wanted so badly to comfort her, but I didn't know how. What could I say or do to make her feel better? All I knew how to do was sew, and yet I needed her to know that I saw her pain.

So, I did the very best I could with the talents I have. I made her a quilt. When I gave it to her, I told her, "I don't know what to say. I don't know how to change anything. I don't even know how to feel what you feel. So I'm hoping that you'll find love and comfort in wrapping this around yourself."

We never know how someone is going to receive a quilt. The impact can be smaller than you expect, or it can be greater than you'll ever realize. Sometimes it's a source of comfort, sometimes it's emotional relief, sometimes they're touched simply by being noticed. All we can do is put our heart into what we make and trust that the quilt will find a way to deliver whatever that person needs at the time. I don't know if the quilt I made actually comforted my friend. We never talked about it after the fact. But it was what I could do. And it was enough.

In the end, I gave with my heart. I didn't have to do anything but that, and neither do you. You don't even have to quilt. Whatever your talent is, it's enough. If it's writing, then write down your feelings or compose a poem for them. If you sing or clean or listen—regardless of what your talent is, it's enough to give it with your heart.

Family and Loss

Loss doesn't discriminate. It doesn't care about your age, race, or social status. Loss comes for all of us at one time or another—a truth that is both comforting and terrifying.

I lost my parents slowly. My mother survived a stroke in 2012 and spent the last years of her life fighting to regain speech and motor skills. My dad watched her fade from that time on, fading with her until she passed away in 2021. My dad never lived much after Mom passed. He was healthy enough, but his heart had broken.

When I heard she'd passed away, I was at a Doan Girls' Quilting Retreat. The loss stepped into my chest, twisting my heart into knots. After her stroke I'd prepared for my mother's death. As a family, we'd known my mom's time was coming, but when it happened, grief still flooded my whole body. I had to hold it together for my guests, yet alongside my efforts to care for everyone else, I hadn't considered what I would need when I lost her.

Everyone at that retreat wanted to comfort me. Without prompting, they got together, and each made me a quilt block featuring a message written inside a pieced heart. I received quotes and thoughts like "For all the hearts you've touched" and "With gratitude and thanks for all you do." There were blocks like that from every person. It was very special to receive such a personal gift. I turned those hearts into a quilt that I still keep in my room.

Those beautiful blocks hold a poignant place in my memory and heart, but it wasn't the words or the sewing that helped me heal. I was the recipient of intentional love from sympathetic women that day. I had forgotten that sometimes it's important to let people take care of me. We all forget this truth on occasion, but that day I was reminded through their efforts that I wasn't alone. My struggles were seen and accepted.

They showed me, on a personal level, how much it matters to give what we can.

Even if all we do is sew.

I recently encountered the story of a grieving woman I follow online. I don't know her personally, but she was familiar, and she made a tearful post about having lost her husband. Well, it was more than tearful. Her words were raw, ugly, and open. I connected deeply as her tender emotions drew me in. Her grieving became so real, I could see myself in it.

Her process of grief taught me about myself. In a similar circumstance I think I would grieve like that—openly, with my heart on my sleeve and a bucket for my tears. But it was seeing her come through that brutal pain that caught me by surprise.

I remember a particular post she made where she was struggling with guilt. It hadn't been that long since her husband's death, and someone had made her laugh. She was crying about it and confused and frustrated. She didn't understand how she could be laughing without her husband there. I watched that video like I'd been stitched to the screen. I know that guilt and loss. I know how it feels to be so conflicted. She was moving forward without her own consent.

People are resilient. That's a good thing, right? It is . . . until grief turns our strength into a curse. Loss slipping away is its own kind of pain. We call ourselves to judgment for newfound laughter. Guilt taints our experiences as we lose the grip we had on our sadness. Like a needle that's been sharpened on both ends, we have to sew to complete the seam, but no matter how we push the needle through, it hurts.

Too many of us connect personally with that kind of pain. There are experiences in my life where I felt so much grief, I didn't think I'd be able to get through it. At the beginning of my first marriage, I had a very simple plan: start a life with my husband and have a baby. In my mind it was so straightforward. I wasn't prepared for the miscarriages. My first was fairly early in the pregnancy; I almost didn't believe it had happened. I tried again—and miscarried again. And then again.

Over the first years of our marriage, I had miscarriage after miscarriage. Some were early miscarriages, but not all; I lost my babies anywhere from the first trimester to nearly halfway through the pregnancy. I just couldn't seem to keep a baby, and all I could think was, *It was supposed to be simple.*

The most difficult miscarriage I had happened after five months of pregnancy. I lost a little girl. I felt her with me all the time, even after the miscarriage. We had already named her. I was preparing clothes and a room for her. The emotional pain of losing her rivaled the physical pain of my last miscarriage.

That final miscarriage was a tubal pregnancy—it ruptured, leaving me with no ovary and a deformed fallopian tube on one side of my body and half of the remaining ovary on the other side. They told me I would probably never have children.

My dreams of motherhood left me. I had no idea how I would even begin to move on.

Natalie was my first miracle. When I had her, I couldn't believe I'd actually given birth to a baby. She was so sweet, and because this journey hadn't started as easily as I'd expected, I didn't waste a second with her. It helped me never take her for granted.

The difficulty I had bringing Natalie into the world reminded me to be grateful for the smallest things. I had a precious life to take care of.

After Natalie was born it was only a few months before Sarah was on the way. Ten months after her birth, I was pregnant with Hillary. My belief that I wouldn't have children dissipated with each healthy birth. After having two more boys I gave birth to my last baby, Joshua. He was healthy and thriving, but I was not. Physically, I was not handling the pregnancies well, and my body was falling apart . . . literally.

I was only twenty-nine when I had to have a hysterectomy. I was so young, and I loved being pregnant. I thought I looked amazing, and I felt even better—ironic considering how my body reacted to carrying a baby. But I never felt that during the months I was expecting. I loved everything about growing tiny humans. I loved imagining what they were going to look like when they grew up and how they were all so different. The emotional whiplash of not being able to have children, followed by this rush of babies, and then having that possibility taken away again was true grief.

But I couldn't grieve. I didn't have time.

I'd begged God for these babies, and now that I had them, I had to get up and keep going—every single day.

We all have heartbreaking things that happen to us. We suffer, cry, and fall apart. Then we get up. It's as if there's a rule that says, "Regardless of how broken your heart is, you can still go on." And we do. The loss and pain don't go away, but time marches on abruptly without another thought for us. Things keep happening, the focus changes, and we learn to look in a different

Jenny with her parents.

direction. That process changes us. Pain makes us kinder and more empathetic, especially toward people who have experienced those same heartaches.

My babies grew, navigating the minefield of childhood and teen years with the grace of a carnival Whac-A-Mole player. My youngest son seemed prone to injury and drama, to the point that I thought I'd grown callous to his tears. But life has a way of waking us up when we grow complacent. When Joshua was five years old, I ran my hand down his arm while helping him change his shirt. Inside his elbow hid a walnut-sized lump. This wasn't a scrape or bug bite. It was a solid mass under his arm.

I couldn't breathe. Joshua watched my face, his brow puckering, when my smile vanished. I was terrified, but I hid it the best I could. I checked his arm again to make sure I wasn't hallucinating and then sent him to play. There was no way for me to know what it was, except that every shred of knowledge I had told me a lump was bad.

Our bodies are predictable: organized bundles of muscle, skin, and bones. A lump meant disease and possible death.

The phone call to the doctor didn't take long. They saw Joshua within days. We learned that the lump was a tumor in his lymph gland with an unknown growth rate. It was only a matter of weeks between discovering it and having it removed and sending it off to be tested. I felt *very* mortal.

Jenny's parents are Frank and Geraldine (Deannie) Fish.

My mom would call me and ask how I was doing. It was an awful question to ask—and to answer—but she was my mother, and she couldn't ignore what was happening. I didn't know how to tell her about the vacant feeling in my chest or the lingering questions that clung to my vision and tinged my happy-go-lucky world with fear. I can still hear myself answering her.

"Every night I think I'm gonna die of a broken heart. And every day I get up, and I do the dishes, and I do the laundry, and I take care of my children, and we go to the doctor's. We do everything that needs to be done. And then I go to bed, and I cry myself to sleep. I just cry."

That's what fear does. Things that mattered before stopped mattering, and things I never imagined dealing with consumed me. I couldn't bear the thought of losing a child, but the fear of cancer and death was so real. Subconsciously, I planned what his room would become without him in it. I planned what I would do with his things if we learned he was sick. I had to prepare. They weren't able to determine what the lump was at the time, and in our financial situation we couldn't push the testing. So they didn't say, and we didn't know. Waiting and watching, we assumed the worst.

In the end we were blessed to find out Joshua would be fine, but it took months to learn that. During that time, the loss felt so finite. The possibility of losing a baby that I'd begged for and again going through grief shredded the fabric of my heart.

There have been many times when I've stood looking at the scattered pieces of my heart, wondering if they'll ever come together again. Loss weaves its fingers through my life, plucking at friends and family members, and each time I think I've figured out how to deal with it. I'm familiar with grief; I may even wallow in it for a while, and that's okay. But then I figure out how to survive. I figure out how to move on. Because we are meant to be happy—we are here to have joy. Resilience is neither a curse nor a gift; it's where hope comes from. We decide what it will do in our lives, and eventually, we find ourselves laughing or chuckling about something. Guilt might creep in at the thought of moving on so soon, but grief is not the end. It's a pathway.

Through all the pain that comes, I know I'll move on. There will be many things to laugh about, and I will find joy again. I just will. I've been through enough sorrow to know life continues. And that's a beautiful thing.

Quilting Through Grief

Grief looks different for everyone, but we have all been given the means to heal and grow from our deepest heartaches. And I've been inspired to see how people have used quilting to heal hearts and lives.

I had never heard of a rainbow baby before I met a quilter in our shop who shared her experience with me. She explained that a *rainbow baby* was the baby someone had following a miscarriage, and she'd designed a quilt she called a *Rainbow Quilt* to express her loss and love.

There's a charity of women who make quilts for stillborn babies that have never taken a breath. The expression of love and caring in those quilts is for both the baby and parents as they experience birth and death in a moment. The parents can wrap their child in a quilt before they say goodbye, and the babies get swaddled in a piece of the love they deserve.

When parents or grandparents become bedridden or confined to a wheelchair, it's a sweet time to make a quilt to brighten their rooms and bring a little happiness. My parents were homebound for years before they passed. I made them flannel quilts for winter and lighter ones for summer. I made a quilt that was all fish for my dad and a Swedish quilt for my mother. When my daughter's father-in-law went into memory care with dementia, I made him a quilt with football fabric from his favorite team, the Kansas City Chiefs, so he could sit under it and watch the games. It's important for us to create things to comfort and celebrate people and their lives.

Ron's mother died of Alzheimer's while we lived states away. Even before she passed, he struggled through the familiar stages of grief as he worried about and tried to care for his parents from afar. He had helpful siblings who lived closer, and his father was still able to help care for his mother, but Ron wanted to be there.

Ron's mother could only remember a collection of moments and years. The difficulty became not only looking out for her physical care but helping her cope with the fear and displacement her condition brought.

I couldn't take Ron's grief away, no matter how much I wanted to. Grief helps us heal. It scabs over the raw pain of loss and creates a barrier of therapeutic memory and truth. It becomes scaffolding to lift and bear the burden of loss. Ron's grief bore him through the pain of losing first his mother, then his father, and eventually his brother. My grief buffered me through my own losses, cradling the pain of trauma in not just heartache but love.

Years later I created a quilt in Ron's mother's honor, using a template for the forget-me-not flower (the official Alzheimer's flower) as a focal point, and paired it with a patchwork block. We titled it *Missing You*. It was released during Alzheimer's Awareness Month.

We had another cancer scare in our family not too long ago, and I was concerned that a quilt wouldn't be enough. I again began to question what I could do to help, and my self-doubt stopped me from doing what I do best. As soon as I realized that, I started to sew. I wanted to send love and comfort, so I made a star-covered quilt in colors I knew they liked. The stars proclaimed words of power like "Brave," "Fight," and "Peace" in the center of each block.

As I sent it off, my worries returned. What if it wasn't the right thing? What if it wasn't appreciated? I had to remind myself that it's not about receiving the greatest gift. It's about me giving love the way I know how.

I didn't have to worry. The quilt arrived in the middle of treatments and doctor visits, and I got a call soon after.

"I curl up in it every day," she told me.

It was a teary phone call, though I'm not sure if they were my tears or hers. I felt like I'd climbed Mount Everest. The quilt had worked its magic. It gave her what she needed: love. Love is always worthwhile.

TENDER HEARTS QUILT

he *Tender Hearts* quilt is an easy way to make heart quilt blocks. Stack them up or scatter them across a quilt top to share with someone who needs a little extra love. Maybe it's you! The hearts in this quilt indicate love, and that's what you're putting into your quilts. So, as you create, keep the people or person you're sewing for in mind, because when you give with your heart, their heart feels it.

Project Info

Quilt Size
72" x 77"

Block Size
9 1/2" x 8 1/2" unfinished,
   9" x 8" finished

Supply List

Quilt Top
1 roll of 2 1/2" print strips
2 1/2 yards of background
   fabric (includes inner
   border and cornerstones)
1 1/2 yards of contrasting solid
   for sashing rectangles

Outer Border
1 1/2 yards

Binding
3/4 yard

Backing
4 3/4 yards for vertical seam(s) or 2 1/2 yards of 108" wide

1 Cut

From the background fabric, cut:

- (8) 5″ strips across the width of the fabric. Subcut each strip into (8) 5″ squares for a **total of 60** squares. There will be 4 squares left over. Cut (2) 2½″ squares from one of the leftovers. Add these to the squares to be set aside for cornerstones. (See next cutting instruction.)
- (17) 2½″ strips across the width of the fabric. Subcut 10 strips into (16) 2½″ squares for a **total of 160** squares. Set the remaining 7 strips aside for the inner border. Set 42 squares aside for the cornerstones. (Be sure to include the 2 squares you cut from the leftover 5″ squares.)

From the contrasting solid fabric, cut (18) 2½″ strips across the width of the fabric.

Subcut 9 strips into 2½″ x 9½″ rectangles for the horizontal sashing rectangles for a **total of 64** rectangles.

Subcut the remaining strips into 2½″ x 8½″ rectangles for the vertical sashing rectangles for a **total of 36** rectangles.

2 Make Strip Sets

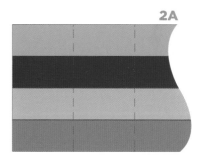

2A

Choose 4 contrasting strips from the roll. Sew the strips together along the long sides. **Make 8** strip sets. Set the remaining strips aside for another project.

Subcut each strip set into (8) 5″ x 8½″ rectangles for a **total of 64** strip-pieced rectangles. **2A**

3 Block Construction—Snowball Corners

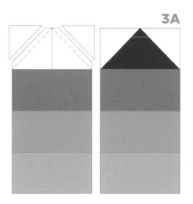

3A

Fold (4) 2½″ background squares once on the diagonal and press the crease in place to mark a sewing line. Place a creased 2½″ background square on one corner of a 5″ x 8½″ strip-pieced rectangle with right sides facing. Stitch on the sewing line, then trim the excess fabric ¼″ away from the sewn seam.

Repeat for the adjacent side of the rectangle. **3A**

Make 2 and sew them together vertically as shown. **3B**

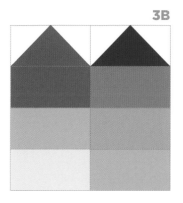

3B

Fold (2) 5″ background squares once on the diagonal and press the crease in place to mark a sewing line. Place a creased 5″ background square atop one lower corner of the block with right sides facing. Sew on the marked sewing line. Move the piece over ½″ from the sewn seam and stitch another seam line.

Repeat for the adjacent lower corner of the block.

Using your rotary cutter, cut between the two sewn seams. Open the corners and press the seam allowances toward the darker fabric. **Make 30** blocks. **3C**

Set the 60 bonus half-square triangles aside to use when making the table Tender Hearts Table Runner. (You will find the pattern on page 114).

Block Size: 9 1/2" x 8 1/2" unfinished, 9" x 8" finished

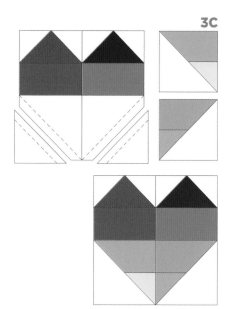

4 Arrange and Sew

Lay out the blocks in **6 rows of 5**. Add a 2 1/2" x 8 1/2" solid sashing rectangle between each block and at the end of each row as shown. Sew the blocks and rectangles together to complete each row. **4A**

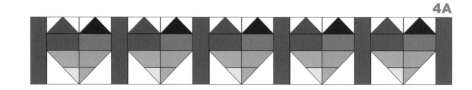

Sew a solid 2 1/2" x 9 1/2" rectangle to a 2 1/2" background square, add a 2 1/2" background square, then another 2 1/2" x 9 1/2" rectangle. Continue on in this manner until you have a strip that consists of (6) 2 1/2" background squares and (5) 2 1/2" x 9 1/2" sashing rectangles. **Make 7** sashing strips. **4B**

Sew the rows together, adding a sashing strip between each row. Add a sashing strip to the top and to the bottom to complete the center of the quilt. (See diagram on page 111).

5 Inner Border

Pick up the (7) 2 1/2" background strips you set aside for the inner border. Sew the strips together end to end to make one long strip. Trim the borders from this strip. **5A**

Refer to Borders (page 181) in the Construction Basics to measure and cut the inner borders. The strips are approximately 62 1/2" for the sides and approximately 61 1/2" for the top and bottom.

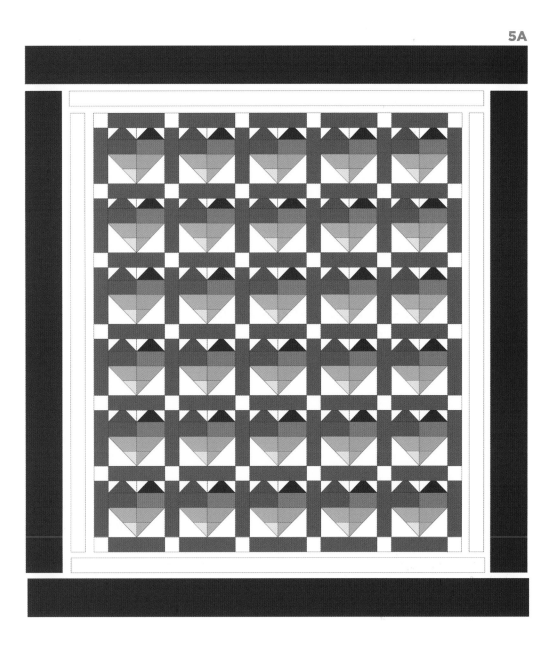

6 Outer Border

From the outer border fabric cut (7) 6″ strips across the width of the fabric. Sew the strips together end to end to make one long strip. Trim the borders from this strip.

Refer to Borders (page 181) in the Construction Basics to measure and cut the outer borders. The strips are approximately 66 ½″ for the sides and approximately 72 ½″ for the top and bottom.

7 Quilt and Bind

Layer the quilt with batting and backing, then quilt. After the quilting is complete, square up the quilt and trim away all excess batting and backing. Add binding to complete the quilt. See Construction Basics (page 182) for binding instructions.

TENDER HEARTS
BONUS PROJECT

TABLE RUNNER

Project Info

Table Runner Size
21" x 35"

Block Size
7 1/2" x 4" unfinished,
    7" x 3 1/2" finished

Supply List

Table Runner Top
60 bonus half-square triangles
    from the *Tender Hearts* quilt

Binding
1/2 yard

Backing
1 yard

1 Block Construction

Open and press the 60 bonus half-square triangles. Press the seam allowances toward the darker fabric. Square each half-square triangle to 4″. Sew 2 half-square triangles together to complete 1 block. **Make 30** blocks. **1A**

Sew 3 blocks together to make one horizontal row. **Make 10** rows. **1B**

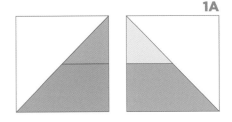

1A

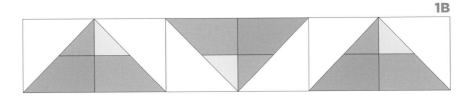

1B

Sew the rows together to complete the table runner. **1C**

1C

2 Quilt and Bind

Layer the table runner with batting and backing, then quilt. After the quilting is complete, square it up and trim away all excess batting and backing. Add binding to complete the project. See Construction Basics (page 182) for binding instructions.

MISSING YOU QUILT

The *Missing You* **quilt** is a simple quilt of patchwork squares around the official Alzheimer's flower, the forget-me-not. I made this quilt in honor of Ron's mother, who had Alzheimer's, and to show support for Alzheimer's Awareness Month (November).

The pattern is designed with a single petal template and a quick patchwork trick, making this pattern simple but special. Alzheimer's affects too many families in this world, and whether you make this quilt because you have lost someone to Alzheimer's or lost who they used to be, I hope you're able to remember that you're not alone. In fact, you're far from it.

Project Info

Quilt Size
75" x 83"

Block Size
12 ½" unfinished, 12" finished

Supply List

Quilt Top
1 package of 10" print squares
¼ yard of orange print fabric
4 yards of background fabric
    (includes inner border)

Outer Border
1 ½ yards

Binding
¾ yard

Backing
2 ¾ yards 90" Cuddle fabric, 5 ¼ yards of 42" wide fabric for vertical seam(s) or 2 ½ yards of
    108" wide

Other:
Missouri Star Petal Template Medium (included; see page 123)
2 packages of Missouri Star Sew Light Fusible Adhesive—17" x 2 yards

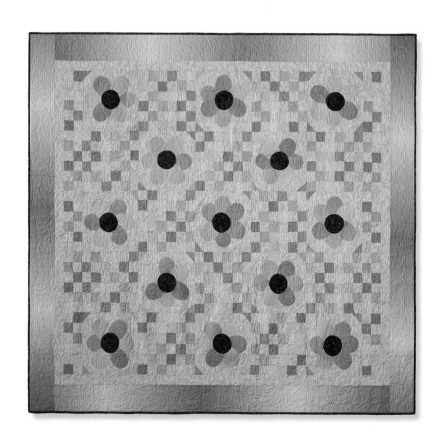

1 Cut and Sort

NOTE: You can set (3) 10" print squares aside or use your whole package for added variety.

From each of your 10" print squares, cut:
- (2) 2 1/2" x 10" strips across the width of each square. A **total of 69** strips are needed.
- (1) 2 1/2" strip along the remaining length of each square to yield (1) 2 1/2" x 5" strip and (1) 5" x 7 1/2" rectangle. Subcut each of the 2 1/2" x 5" strips in half to yield 2 1/2" squares for a **total of 52** squares. Set the 5" x 7 1/2" print rectangles aside for the petals.

From the background fabric, cut:
- (5) 12 1/2" strips across the width of fabric. Subcut:
  - 4 strips into (3) 12 1/2" squares each.
  - 1 strip into (1) 12 1/2" square. Add the square to your other 12 squares for a **total of 13** squares, and trim the remainder of the strip into (5) 2 1/2" strips across the width of the remaining fabric.
- (31) 2 1/2" strips across the width of the fabric. Add 24 strips to the 5 strips cut previously. Set 7 strips aside for the inner border.

From the fusible interfacing, cut:
- (20) 5" strips across the width of the interfacing. Subcut the strips into 5" x 7 1/2" rectangles for a **total of 39** rectangles.
- (2) 8 1/2" strips across the width of the interfacing.

2 Sew 36-Patch Blocks

Sew a 2 1/2" x 10" print strip to a 2 1/2" background strip, right sides facing. Take a few stitches past the end of the print strip and add another print strip to chain-piece them together. Continue until you reach the end of the background strip. **2A**

Trim the 2 1/2" x 10" strip sets apart. **2B**

Select 3 strip sets with different prints and sew them together as shown. Press all the seams toward the top. **Make 23** strip set units. **2C**

Cut each strip set unit into (4) 2 1/2" x 12 1/2" segments for a **total of 92** segment strips. **2D**

Select 6 pieced strips with different fabrics and arrange them in a checkerboard pattern as shown. Notice how every other segment strip is rotated 180° from the last and the

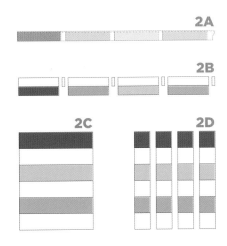

seams nest when rotated properly. Sew them together, then press. Square to 12 1/2″ if needed. **Make 12** blocks.

Set the rest of the segment strips aside for the checkerboard sashing rows. **2E 2F**

3 Fuse and Cut

Follow the manufacturer's instructions to adhere the interfacing to the wrong sides of the 5″ x 7 1/2″ print rectangles. Use the template to cut petals from the rectangles. Cut a **total of 78** petals.

Using the circle template on page 123 or a jar lid that is 3 1/2″ to 4″ in diameter, trace 13 circles onto the 8 1/2″ fusible interfacing strips and adhere as before to the wrong side of the orange print fabric. Cut a **total of 13** circles.

4 Sew Flower Blocks

Lightly press a 12 1/2″ background square in half both ways to make centering creases. **4A**

Arrange 6 fused petals as shown. Adhere the petals following the manufacturer's instructions. Add the flower center in the same manner. Appliqué the petals and flower center using a blanket stitch or small zigzag stitch. **Make 13** flower blocks. **4B 4C**

Mark a diagonal line on the reverse side of (52) 2 1/2″ print squares. **4D**

Place a marked square on all 4 corners of a flower block, right sides facing, as shown. Pin the squares in place and sew on the lines. Trim 1/4″ past the seams and press to make snowballed corners. Repeat with all of the flower blocks. **4E 4F**

5 Make Checkerboard Sashing Rows

Sew 5 segment strips you set aside earlier together end to end as shown. **Make 4** strips. **5A 5B**

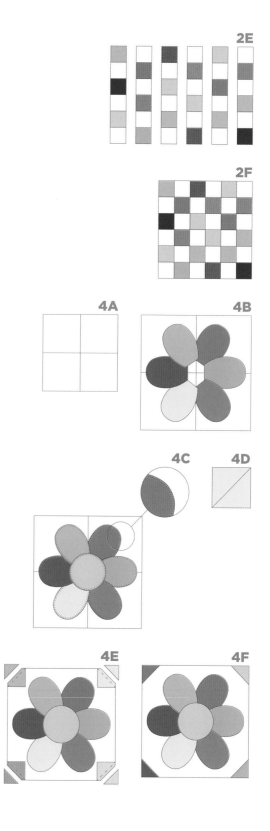

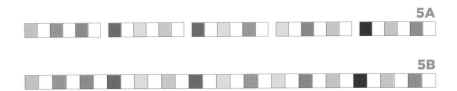
5A

5B

Arrange 2 rows of strips, 1 above the other, rotating the bottom strip so the colors alternate in a checkerboard pattern. Sew the rows together and press. **Make 2** checkerboard sashing rows. **5C**

5C

6 Arrange and Sew

Arrange the blocks into **5 rows of 5** as shown in the diagram on page 122. Sew the blocks together to form rows. Press in opposite directions. Nest the seams and sew the rows together.

Sew a checkerboard sashing row to the top and bottom of the quilt top. Note the placement of the background squares in the checkerboard sashing rows. Press. **6A**

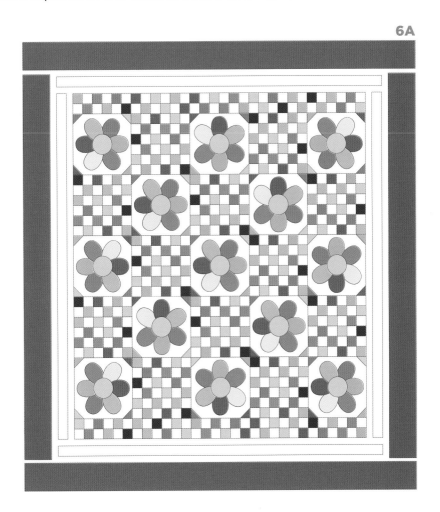
6A

7 Inner Border

Gather the (7) 2 1/2″ background strips set aside earlier and sew them together to make one long strip. Trim the borders from this strip.

Refer to Borders (page 181) in the Construction Basics to measure, cut, and attach the borders. The lengths are approximately 68 1/2″ for the sides and 64 1/2″ for the top and bottom.

8 Outer Border

Cut (8) 6″ strips across the width of the outer border fabric. Sew the strips together to make one long strip. Trim the borders from this strip.

Refer to Borders (page 181) in the Construction Basics to measure, cut, and attach the borders. The lengths are approximately 72 1/2″ for the sides and 75 1/2″ for the top and bottom.

9 Quilt and Bind

Layer the quilt with batting and backing, then quilt. After the quilting is complete, square up the quilt and trim away all excess batting and backing. Add binding to complete the quilt. See Construction Basics (page 182) for binding instructions.

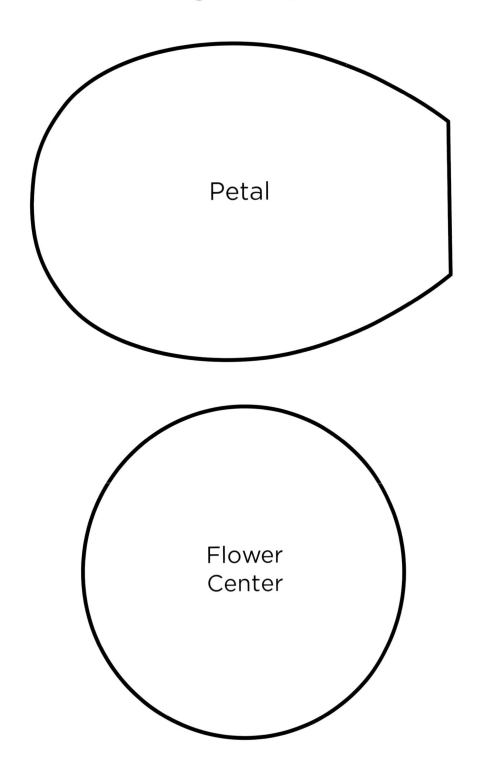

Petal

Flower
Center

DISAPPEARING PINWHEEL
CHURN DASH QUILT

When is a pinwheel not a pinwheel? Simple—when it's a churn dash. In the *Disappearing Pinwheel Churn Dash Quilt*, we illustrate how completely loss changes us by taking a beautiful pinwheel block that changes with a simple pattern as you work the fabric. With a few carefully chosen cuts and a bit of rearranging, the loss of one block leads to something new, minus the grief.

Project Info

Quilt Size
57" x 68"

Block Size
12 1/4" unfinished,
    11 3/4" finished

Supply List

Quilt Top
1 package of 10" print squares

Outer Border
1 1/2 yards

Binding
3/4 yard

Backing
3 3/4 yards for horizontal
    seam(s)

1 Make Half-Square Triangles

Sort the 10″ squares into 10 high-contrast pairs and 10 low-contrast pairs.

Layer the light square atop the dark square, right sides facing. Sew around the perimeter. **1A**

Cut the sewn squares twice diagonally. Open and press. Each set of sewn squares will yield 4 half-square triangles. Repeat with the remaining pairs to **yield 80** units. **1B**

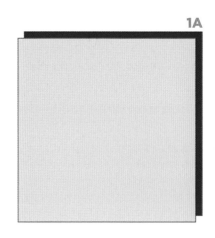

2 Make Pinwheels

Arrange 4 half-square triangles as shown to form a pinwheel. **2A**

Sew the top 2 units into a row and press the seam in one direction. Sew the bottom 2 units and press the seam in the opposite direction. Nesting the seams, sew the two rows together and press the seams open. **Make 20** pinwheels.

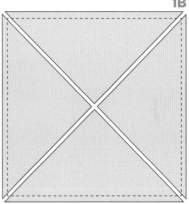

3 Assemble the Blocks

Measure and cut 2 ⅛″ from both horizontal and vertical center seams—on both sides of the seams, turning the block without disturbing it. **3A**

Rotate the top and bottom center units 90° counterclockwise and the left and right center units 90° clockwise. Turn the corner units so the dark fabric tip is facing the center.

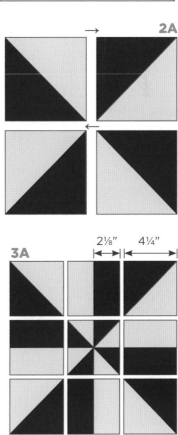

Sew the units together in each row, pressing the seams in opposite directions. Sew the rows together and press the seams open. **Make 10** blocks. **3B**

Block size: 12 1/4″ unfinished, 11 3/4″ finished

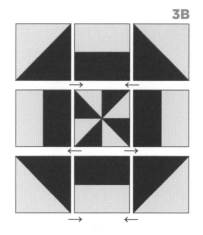

4 Arrange and Sew

Refer to the diagram to lay out the blocks in **4 rows of 5**. Sew the blocks together to form rows. Press the seams in opposite directions. Nest the seams, sew the rows together, and then press to complete the quilt top. **4A**

5 Border

Cut (7) 6″ strips across the width from the border fabric. Sew the strips together to make a long strip. Trim the borders from this strip.

Refer to Borders (page 181) in the Construction Basics to measure, cut, and attach the borders. The strip lengths are approximately 59 $\frac{1}{2}$″ for the sides and 58 $\frac{1}{2}$″ for the top and bottom.

6 Quilt and Bind

Layer the quilt with batting and backing, then quilt. After the quilting is complete, see Construction Basics (page 182) to add binding and finish your quilt.

COURTHOUSE STEPS QUILT

The courthouse steps are quite literally home to many losses. I've finalized divorce there and seen people lose homes and more there. You can make the *Courthouse Steps* quilt in bright (or soothing, if you prefer) colors. Either way, don't ignore these steps in your life, but hang on. It's not the end. It really does get easier as you move forward into this new pattern of your life.

Project Info

Quilt Size
76" x 76"

Block Size
14 1/2" unfinished, 14" finished

Supply List

Quilt Top
1 roll of 2 1/2" print strips
1 roll of 2 1/2" background strips

First and Third Borders
3/4 yard

Outer Border
1 1/2 yards

Binding
3/4 yard

Backing
4 3/4 yards for vertical seam(s) or 2 1/2 yards of 108" wide

1 Cut

> **TIP:** In order to make the most of your fabric, cut the longest strips first.

From the background roll, cut:
- (16) 2 ½" x 14 ½" strips
- (32) 2 ½" x 10 ½" strips
- (32) 2 ½" x 6 ½" strips
- (24) 2 ½" squares

From the print roll, cut:
- (16) 2 ½" x 14 ½" strips
- (32) 2 ½" x 10 ½" strips
- (32) 2 ½" x 6 ½" strips
- (24) 2 ½" squares

NOTE: All blocks are made the same, but the color placement changes, so we will **make 8** of Block A and **make 8** of Block B.

2 Block A

Sew a 2 ½" print square to both sides of a 2 ½" background square. **2A**

Sew a 2 ½" x 6 ½" background strip to the top and bottom of the unit. **2B**

Add a 2 ½" x 6 ½" print strip to both sides of the unit. **2C**

Sew a 2 ½" x 10 ½" background strip to the top and bottom of the unit. **2D**

Add a 2 ½" x 10 ½" print strip to both sides of the unit. **2E**

Sew a 2 ½" x 14 ½" background strip to the top and bottom of the unit to complete the block. **Make 8** blocks. **2F**

Block Size: 14 ½" unfinished, 14" finished

3 Block B

Sew a 2 ½" background square to both sides of a 2 ½" print square. **3A**

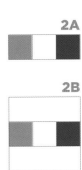
2A

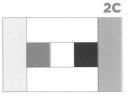
2B

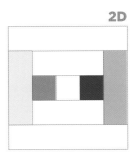
2C

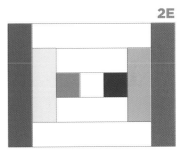
2D

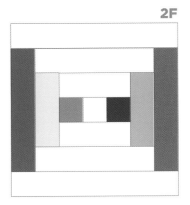
2E

2F

3A

Sew a 2 1/2" x 6 1/2" print strip to top and bottom of the unit. **3B**

Add a 2 1/2" x 6 1/2" background strip to both sides of the unit. **3C**

Sew a 2 1/2" x 10 1/2" print strip to the top and bottom of the unit. **3D**

Add a 2 1/2" x 10 1/2" background strip to both sides of the unit. **3E**

Sew a 2 1/2" x 14 1/2" print strip to the top and bottom of the unit to complete the block. **Make 8** blocks. **3F**

Block Size: 14 1/2" unfinished, 14" finished

4 Arrange and Sew

Lay out the blocks in **4 rows of 4**.

NOTE: Block A is rotated a quarter turn.

Begin row 1 and row 3 with Block B and alternate with Block A. Begin rows 2 and 4 with Block A and alternate with Block B.

Sew the blocks together in rows and press in opposite directions. Nest the seams and sew the rows together. Press.

5 First and Third Borders

Cut (13) 1 1/2" strips across the width of the fabric. Sew the strips together end to end to make one long strip. Trim the first and third borders from this strip.

Refer to Borders (page 181) in the Construction Basics to measure and cut the inner borders. The strips are approximately 56 1/2" for the sides and approximately 58 1/2" for the top and bottom of the first border.

The strips are approximately 63 1/2" for the sides and 65 1/2" for the top and bottom of the third border. **5A**

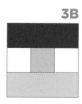

3B

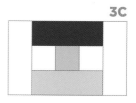

3C

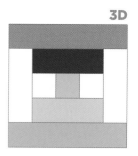

3D

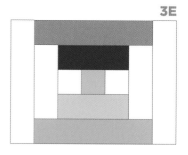

3E

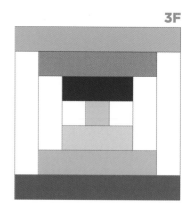

3F

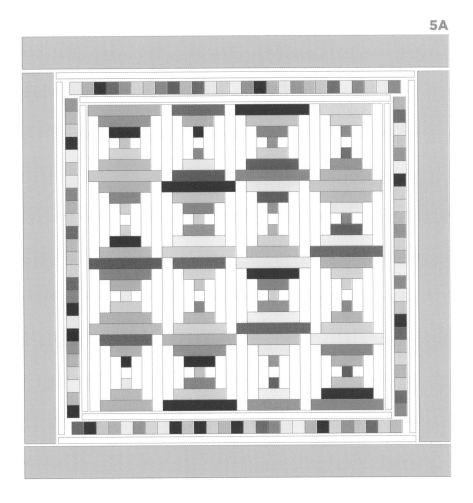

6 Second Border—Pieced

Cut the leftover print strips into 3″ increments for a **total of 122** pieces.

Make a 3″-wide unfinished side border by sewing 29 pieces together. **Make 2** borders and sew 1 to both sides of the quilt.

Sew 32 pieces together. **Make 2** borders. Sew 1 to the top of the quilt and 1 to the bottom.

Refer to Borders (page 181) in the Construction Basics to measure and adjust the pieced borders if necessary. If you find the borders aren't quite working, use a smaller or larger seam allowance to compensate for the measurement being a little off. If you make the adjustments small and do it over several pieces, it won't be noticeable. The strips are approximately 58 1/2″ for the sides and approximately 63 1/2″ for the top and bottom.

7 Outer Border

From the outer border fabric cut (8) 6″ strips across the width of the fabric. Sew the strips together end to end to make one long strip. Trim the outer borders from this strip.

Refer to Borders (page 181) in the Construction Basics to measure and cut the outer border. The strips are approximately 65 1/2″ for the sides and approximately 76 1/2″ for the top and bottom.

8 Quilt and Bind

Layer the quilt with batting and backing, then quilt. After the quilting is complete, square up the quilt and trim away all excess batting and backing. Add binding to complete the quilt. See Construction Basics (page 182) for binding instructions.

CHAPTER 8

THE EMPTY-NEST YEARS AND RETIREMENT

The phrase *empty nester* is a lonely one. It looms unavoidably, just beyond the moment when our children leave us. It's been almost twenty years since Ron and I officially joined these ranks . . . temporarily. Shortly after Joshua moved out, Sarah moved back in. She was having a house built, and during the transition she stayed at our place, along with her family—complete with husband, toddlers, and baby.

I don't know if that was harder on them or us.

Eventually, Sarah's family finished their beautiful home and moved out with all the toys, noise, and children. And we brushed off the empty nester title . . . just as the family of another one of our children moved home. So, we put the term away again, happily denying our new phase of life a little longer. We occasionally tried out the title again between visitors and friends as we attempted to settle into the idea of an empty home.

I'd never used the word *empty* to describe my life before. Frankly, my life has never been empty, and neither has my nest. I've worked with children all my life, mothering my own and then transitioning to work at a school for local teens. I taught kids about their own self-worth for years. All that time I was sewing, but the people around me were growing and breaking away into their own lives. I raised my children to be independent, and when they were, it was harder than I thought it would be.

I have lived most of my life with a the-more-the-merrier mentality. It has kept our home and hearts full, though for a long time it made it harder to consider ourselves true empty nesters.

When we were finally alone for more than a few days at a time, I realized very quickly that I missed my busy house.

The transition into an empty nest had its own bumps. Habits were the first things I noticed changing when our family trimmed down to just the two of us. I had to relearn basic skills like cooking, cleaning, and even shopping. Full bags of pasta are a frustrating reality if you forget that you've downsized your family and cook the entire package of noodles. Dishwashers become a luxury cleaning tool when it suddenly takes days to fill up a single rack of dirty dishes.

Being an empty nester was hard. Ron and I never had the years of alone time most couples have when they're first married. We got married with kids, jumping right into our family. He never complained about it, but now my husband and I had so much time together. Sometimes it was too much time.

With some effort we learned to adapt and enjoy each other's full-time company. And once I remembered how much I liked spending time with him, it became really fun. Now, we spend time doing all sorts of things. Sometimes we're busy with work or helping the kids, but we both have quite a few hobbies as well. We paint, cook, and create while we enjoy each other—usually through vastly different creative endeavors. From my music and theater to his woodworking and motorcycles, we're individual people with individual interests. But if I ask him to, my car guy will become a plant guy to help me out. He moves my houseplants when they get too heavy and waters them any time I ask. This may not mean he's become a plant person, but our hobbies do rub off on each other.

Ron and Jenny on one of their many trips.

For instance, I like building things with him, and Ron has taken up needlework with me! One of the most exciting things is that in my recent embroidery quilts, there are several panels that Ron has done entirely himself. He has been a machinist for most of his life, and because of this profession, he has a great attention to detail and precision that makes his embroidery a collage of tiny, beautiful, uniform stitches. That's something my embroidery only hopes to be. I'm not the most patient of handworkers, and my stitches reflect that. They cover distances quickly, shaping the designs in efficient and speedy stitches that are somewhat less precise than my husband's, but they get the job done.

As the years have passed, I've loved seeing Ron find new ways to express his creativity. We're very different, but we've always worked well together, and now we're doing the same with our quilting. We sit side by side most evenings, him with his project and me with mine. His quilts take ages to finish, and they couldn't be more different than what I am creating. He likes tiny little paper piecing inspired by complex, grayscale photographs. I like straight lines and quick results.

When people see his work, they always ask me, "Did you teach him to do that?"

I hold up whatever pack of precuts I'm working with and shake my head. "Nope. I'm just happy to sew two squares together!"

His quilts amaze me. He amazes me. When he has an idea, he works it down to the tiniest details. He's not afraid of curves and isn't bogged down by technicalities like standard shapes or insecure questions like, "How will it go together?" or "Does that mountain look like a nose?" I'm stunted by those things and shift quickly to problems I can solve.

Because of these changes we've grown into as empty nesters, we've gotten to know each other in a whole new way. We plan and do things differently. I used to think I was the creative one in our relationship, and it took me too long to realize creativity is something we both share. His is quiet and thoughtful, with detailed expressions of beauty that I would never dream of, while I throw creativity around wildly, reveling in the inherent beauty of all things.

Fabric and quilting have always been more than a job to me. It's work I love and projects that mean something. In this new phase of life, sewing has doubled its purpose in my life again. It has eased our transition into empty nesting and become an opportunity for my husband and me to spend time together.

Broccoli and Bucket Lists

For many of us, age sixty-five means retirement. But my empty nest looks different than yours, and my retirement will too. Sixty-five hit me head on recently, and you know, I didn't feel any different that morning than I did at sixty-four years and three hundred and sixty-four days. I still want to work and have hobbies and spend time with my kids and everything I did before. There are also things I don't want to do anymore, like mowing the lawn.

As a younger mom, I used to love mowing the lawn because it got me away from the house and the children for at least forty-five uninterrupted minutes. It was just me and that patch of green. I used to barter with Ron for mowing duty. I'd trade dishes in the air-conditioned house for mowing in the California sun any day. Even though our yard wasn't huge, I loved this outside alone time, and Ron was always happy to trade. He probably knew he was giving me a gift.

Now that I don't need to steal alone time, I've been reexamining what I enjoy. I spend time sewing and weeding. I take creative classes with my daughters. I garden with my sons and talk to my houseplants while I water or repot them.

And I have someone else mow my lawn.

The decision to be okay with disliking something I'd trained myself to do was freeing.

Natalie, Al, Sarah, and Jenny in the first Missouri Quilt Co. shop.

It helped me see myself differently. I am still a hard worker, but mowing the lawn no longer gives me the reward and joy it used to.

Identifying the things you love, and *why* you love them, then letting go of the things you don't love will open your life to joy. Who wants to fill their limited time with survival tactics disguised as happiness? You could be filling your time with truly joyful moments.

When I was forty, I said to Ron, "I don't have to like broccoli anymore. Do I?"

My declaration caught his attention and resulted in a raised eyebrow. "Of course not," he replied.

"Good. Because I don't like broccoli. I didn't like it last year, and I don't think I'll like it next year. No one cares if I like broccoli, and there are chewy, fruit-flavored tablets to get my vitamins."

"That's true." He drew the words out slowly and skeptically. He was probably thinking I'd tipped right off my rocker.

"I think . . . No—" I was still wrapping my brain around the fact that I was rejecting a vegetable. I took a freeing breath and let a wall drop between me and the little green tree. "I've decided I definitely don't like broccoli."

Ron, always the supportive spouse, nodded his head. "All right, don't eat broccoli anymore."

How long have I known I don't like broccoli? Forty years? More? Seeing ourselves as full, unbroken human beings isn't easy, and it's not without a process. What makes your life better, no matter how small? What things used to bother you? How long have you been ignoring and putting up with them? Choose carefully the things you keep in your life. You deserve only the best.

There will be things in your life that you have to do because it makes you a better person or because you care about the people around you. Those come with a different reward. But make sure you do them consciously. When you look around, and your home is silent and empty, with retirement looming ahead, you don't want to realize you've lived your life eating foods you hate and doing chores that aren't worth your time and effort.

Growing old with someone beside you will change some of those choices, and that's okay. Retirement will take almost as many compromises as marriage itself—like when Ron and I go camping. I love tent camping, while Ron's idea of roughing it is a Motel 6. I love the outdoors any way I can get it, be it hiking, the smell of the campfire, the sounds of birds and animals. Ron loves . . . some of that. But mostly he just hates sleeping outside . . . and setting the tent up . . . and the excessive summer heat that turns tents into convection ovens. It's not that I particularly like many of those things either. But they're worth it to me so I can be in the wilderness and savor the outdoors.

Ron and I camped a lot in our younger years, but in retirement, he discovered for himself some of the things he didn't like and really didn't have to do. He didn't want to camp within the torture of a tent. He'd go to the wilderness, he'd smell the smells, and he'd enjoy his time beside me, but he didn't want to sleep there. It hurt and made him grumpy. And he decided he didn't *have* to do it.

What can I say—retirement really does look different for everyone.

But I wanted him with me, so we got creative. As a compromise, we bought a little camper that we decked out with an air conditioner and cute camper curtains and decor. Now, we glamp!

He doesn't sleep on the ground in a stuffy tent, and I don't have to pretend camp and sneak off after campfire songs and before bedtime.

And I'm not there just to sit in a hammock. I want to build a fire and make my own dinner. I want to disconnect from the world. Ron just wants to relax. We fused the different sides of what we love about camping, and now we enjoy the time together.

The majority of our family lives locally, other than one son in California and a daughter just over the border of Missouri, in Arkansas. If we ever need company for hobby time, there is always someone nearby who wants to join us.

Ron teaching the grandkids how to make his famous eclairs.

I paint with my grandkids, have a regular night for sewing with a friend, and my son Jacob will talk plants with me all day. Ron plans a weekly carving session with our oldest granddaughter and loves to ride motorcycles with the grandkids or watch our grandsons race go-carts around the country. He particularly loves to bake, and every Sunday we make treats and take them around to all our nearby children and college-aged grandchildren in exchange for hugs.

Halloween is on both of our lists of things we enjoy. Combined with my sewing, our home feels fullest when we all gather for holidays—and suddenly my empty nest remembers what it's like to be full. Christmas is a favorite, but Halloween is almost as much of a production, if not more. We dress up and decorate everything from the food to the front porch. We plan for the holiday almost a year in advance. On those nights, as many family members as possible join in, and our nest feels less empty than ever.

People have continued to come and go in our home, and my empty nest continually changes around me. The rooms that used to be filled with children's toys and teenage posters have gone through several facelifts.

At first, as rooms cleared, my thought was, *Free space? Yes! I'll get a sewing room—finally!*
But life tends to laugh in the face of our best plans.

I've always sewn at the dining room table, surrounded by my family. Now that our house is quieting down . . . I still sew in the dining room. A secluded room upstairs away from the world was like putting on blinders for my creativity. I missed that connection. So, my planned sewing room morphed into a guest room, then back to a sewing room. We tried making a workout room, but that didn't last, so it became a computer room/study, and then a sewing room again. I did my best, but no matter how much I tried, I couldn't make a sewing room stick. That room transitioned several more times until it ended where it started: a simple bedroom.

It shouldn't have surprised me. I have a tendency to gather people, and with as many people as we have had shuffle through our nest, a guest room is what we need.

I'm still not certain my extra rooms are done changing. I'm enjoying them for what they are right now. But I'm not retired yet, and there is so much I still want to do.

It's not only my house that could still be changing. There's so much to be grateful for at this stage of life. I feel like I have the opportunity to choose my future. The shock of our empty nest has subsided and turned into joy at being together with Ron. I've sent my kids into the world, and for the first time in my adult life, the biggest dreams I have to worry about are mine.

Don't waste this time. It's a gift we have to give ourselves. Don't stop doing what you love. Do it differently if you must, but don't stop!

There are ladies who come to our quilt shops on scooters, and they'll apologize for being in the way or causing a challenge, and I'll say, "Don't you dare. You are inspiring!"

These women put in so much effort to get here. They're still traveling and living. If getting out means you have to ride on a scooter, bring that scooter. If there are things you still want to do but you can only get there with a walker, then walk proudly with your walker. Don't be embarrassed to use an aid for your health. We'll all be there one day. You are winning the race. You are not giving up; you are living empowered! It's an attitude of joy and strength.

Jenny and Ron (on couch) and (left to right) Al, Sarah, Natalie, Jake, and Misty at the re-opening of the main shop in 2016.

I'm willing to bet that every single person reading this has places they haven't seen and things they haven't done. Maybe you call it a *bucket list*, maybe you don't, but mine was never very big. I had to learn it was okay to dream before I even knew what to do with a bucket list.

Only a few years after creating our company, I was certain I'd outlived my usefulness. I'd done everything I could to help the business. I'd made some tutorials and gotten things started, but I had daughters to take it over, and the quilt company was bringing on young, new employees with bright, shiny ideas. I couldn't hang around forever, and I figured it was only a matter of time before someone asked me when I would retire. That possibility came into focus when I was invited to go to Alaska!

Why Alaska, you may ask? Well, Alaska was on my *bucket* list. But not just on, it was the whole thing. Going there was the only adventure I'd ever dreamed about. And it was completely out of reach . . . until it wasn't.

So I went to Alaska. I traveled with my husband to give a quilt trunk show and then toured for a couple of days. It was everything I'd hoped it would be.

When I came home, I told my kids how incredible the trip had been. I felt like I'd accomplished everything I was meant to do in this life. So, I gathered my courage and told them my plan. I'd accomplished my dreams, and now I could retire.

I'm lucky they didn't laugh—or worse, agree with me.

They told me I couldn't retire yet . . . and that I needed a bigger bucket list.

They still wanted me around.

I was shocked, but so were my kids—for different reasons, of course. Their love and faith motivated me as I did some soul-searching. *I believe in dreaming big*, I told myself. And when I realized that, for so long, I'd kept myself from doing just that, everything changed. That's when I really started to dream. I *could* go anywhere I wanted to.

My bucket list grew faster than an exploding pineapple block.

This is a time of slowing down, not stopping. So slow down and enjoy life. Create what you love. You can do anything; you just have to be willing to make the sacrifice. If your bucket list looks like it has "$$$" next to it, start setting aside money. It's not too late to save five dollars a week. Or maybe you can do twenty-five. Whatever you can do is amazing! Every trip and adventure will become doable.

I can't begin to tell you how exciting it was when Ron and I started to travel—sometimes for work and quilt shows, sometimes for fun. I felt sparks fly as my bucket list grew, and I invited Ron on every adventure that I could.

I quickly realized I didn't know what Ron had on his bucket list. This was how far off these dreams had been. We'd never even discussed them. So, in an effort to be sure I wasn't keeping him from filling his own bucket list, I asked what he wanted to do.

"Whatever you want to do is fine with me," he said.

Back row: Al, Ron, Seth, Josh; front row: Jenny, Sarah, Natalie, Misty, and Jake at Missouri Star's Seventh Birthday Bash in 2015.

His bucket list was apparently even shorter than mine. He didn't even have a list.

"Yeah . . ." I was certain I could pull an idea out of him. "But don't you want to go to—"

"No. Whatever you want to do is fine with me."

The fact that he really wants to do whatever I want to do is one of the sweetest qualities about this man. But Ron's a few years older than I am, and I wanted to honor his retirement. So, I thought about his interests and suggested some different places. That's what it started with.

"Why don't we go here?" I asked.

"Is that something you want?"

"Well, I think you'd like it, and I would definitely enjoy it."

"All right," he would say. "Let's go there."

It wasn't until after we started doing some things that I saw his eyes light up.

"You know, I'd really like to see . . ."

And that was when we went to Germany. There was a play in Germany that only happens once every ten years, and Ron didn't want to risk missing it. It's a sort of awakening when you learn how big your dreams can be.

I'm looking forward to retiring—I am—but not yet. I want to change, not to quit doing something I love. When my parents passed away, I knew right away I didn't want to handle my life in the same way. So I made a change. I decided I'd do things differently. I wanted to travel more. And quilt more. I was prepared to take life by the shoulders and shake it.

Hillary, Natalie, Jenny, and Ron are all smiles in the rain.

Once again, quilting changed my plans, and it changed our story. I've been blessed to travel around the world to share my love of this craft. It's different than I thought and in some ways even better. I get to do what I love. Sewing fills me. It's a part of me. And I'm going to continue doing it.

Whether I'm sixty-five or eighty-five, there will always be a sewing machine within arm's reach for me. It's the experience I want to keep for the entirety of my life. I will continue quilting into and after retirement, forever and ever.

That bucket list is big enough for me.

JENNY'S TENT
QUILT

If you've ever camped with a family, small or large, you know how much effort it is just to get out the door. But camping was one of our favorite summer vacations. We loved it. We always went somewhere near a river or with short hikes nearby to adventure on. The kids made best friends with one another as they played in the dirt, found secret fairy homes in meadows, and watched for birds and squirrels to name and make friends with. At night, we sang around the campfire and roasted marshmallows.

Jenny's Tent was made in memory of all those nights spent lying on a quilt, looking at the stars. Each block in this quilt looks like a little tent. I could say there is one for every night I spent camping, but if that were true, it would be a much larger quilt!

Project Info

Quilt Size
59" x 67"

Block Size
4 ½" unfinished, 4" finished

Supply List

Quilt Top
1 package of 10" print squares
1 package of 5" neutral squares
    or 1 yard of neutral fabric

Inner Border
½ yard

Outer Border
1 yard

Binding
¾ yard

Backing
3 ¾ yards for horizontal seam(s)

1 Cut

Cut each of the 5″ squares in half twice, once vertically, once horizontally to make a **total of (168)** 2 ½″ squares. **1A**

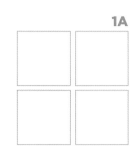

1A

2 Block Construction

Separate the 10″ squares into two stacks. One of light fabrics and the other of darks. On the reverse side of each light square, draw a line from corner to corner twice on the diagonal. **2A**

2A

Place a light square atop a dark square with right sides facing. Sew ¼″ on either side of the drawn lines. **2B**

After you are done sewing, cut the half-square triangle units apart by cutting the squares in half vertically, then horizontally. Then cut on the drawn lines. Press the seam allowance, then open each and press again with the seam allowance going toward the darker fabric. Trim each unit to 4 ½″. **2C**

Fold and press each neutral 2 ½″ square in half with right sides facing. The crease will be your sewing line. **2D**

Stitch a neutral 2 ½″ square to the darkest side of a half-square triangle with right sides facing. Sew on the creased line. Trim the excess fabric away ¼″ from the seam allowance. Press the seam allowance toward the dark fabric. You will need a **total of 168** blocks. **2E**

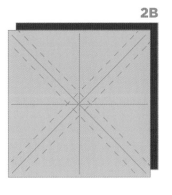

2B

Block Size: 4 ½″ unfinished, 4″ finished

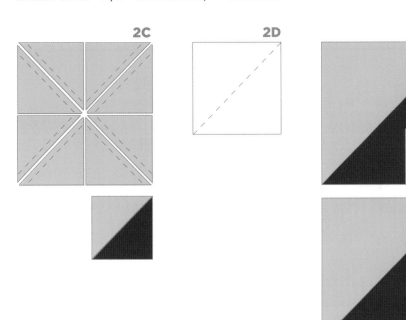

2C

2D

2E

3 Arrange and Sew

Sew the blocks together into rows. Each row consists of **12 blocks**. **Make 14** rows. **3A**

3A

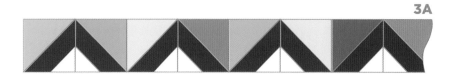

Press seams in opposite directions. Nest the seams, and sew the rows together. Press to complete the center of the quilt top. **3B**

3B

4 Inner Border

From the inner border fabric cut (6) 2 1/2" strips across the width of the fabric. Sew the strips together end to end to make one long strip. Trim the inner borders from this strip.

Refer to Borders (page 181) in the Construction Basics to measure and cut the inner borders. The strips are approximately 56 1/2" for the sides and approximately 52 1/2" for the top and bottom.

5 Outer Border

From the outer border fabric, cut (7) 4" strips across the width of the fabric. Sew the strips together end to end to make one long strip. Trim the outer borders from this strip.

Refer to Borders (page 181) in the Construction Basics to measure and cut the outer borders. The strips are approximately 60 1/2" for the sides and approximately 59 1/2" for the top and bottom.

6 Quilt and Bind

Layer the quilt with batting and backing, then quilt. After the quilting is complete, square up the quilt and trim away all excess batting and backing. Add binding to complete the quilt. See Construction Basics (page 182) for binding instructions.

PAPER STORIES QUILT (JENNY'S PERSONAL CAMPER QUILT)

The *Paper Stories* quilt celebrates my idea of retirement—camping, hiking, and traveling. That is not Ron's idea of slowing down and enjoying life. We bought our camper when Ron retired, and I made this quilt for the bed inside.

Do you remember my advice? Whatever enables you to keep doing what you love, *do it*. Stopping only ages us faster. This quilt helped us make that change more comfortable—literally and metaphorically.

The camper has become a staple in our quick getaways. Being able to enjoy weekends away or sleep comfortably on a family camping trip has encouraged our kids to acquire campers as well. I guess you don't have to be retired to enjoy one! Now we all have our favorite camper quilts to share.

Make one for your adventures while you slow down, relax, and experience every bit of beauty under the stars!

Project Info

Quilt Size
61 ½" x 71"

Block Size
10" unfinished, 9 ½" finished

Supply List

Quilt Top
1 roll of 2 ½" print strips
1 ½ yards of background fabric
　　(includes inner border)

Outer Border
1 ¼ yards

Binding
¾ yard

Backing
4 ½ yards for vertical seam(s)
　　or 2 yards of 108" wide

Other
1 package of Missouri Star 10" Paper Piecing Squares

1 Cut

From the background fabric, cut (21) 2 ½" strips across the width of the fabric. Set 6 strips aside for the inner border.

2 Block Construction

Apply a bit of glue diagonally across the center of your foundation paper. Place a 2 ½" background strip on top, right side up. Lay another piece of fabric on top of the first, right sides together, and align 1 edge. Trim off the excess fabric past the edge of the paper template. Sew along the edge using a ¼" seam allowance. **2A**

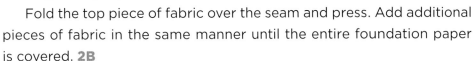

Fold the top piece of fabric over the seam and press. Add additional pieces of fabric in the same manner until the entire foundation paper is covered. **2B**

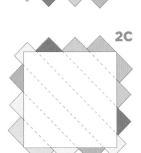

Once the foundation paper is completely covered, turn your block over so the paper is on top. Use the paper as a guide to trim the excess fabric from the block. **2C**

Remove the paper from the back of the block and discard. **Make 30** blocks. **2D**

Block Size: 10" unfinished, 9 ½" finished

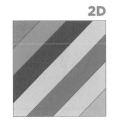

3 Arrange and Sew

Lay the blocks out in **6 rows of 5**. Turn the blocks so that the center background strip forms a diamond shape when 4 blocks come together. The background strips are not meant to match perfectly.

Sew the blocks together side to side to build a row. Press the seams in opposite directions. Nest the seams, and sew the rows together. Press to complete the quilt center. **3A**

4 Inner Border

Pick up the (6) 2 ½" strips you set aside earlier. Sew the strips together end to end to make one long strip. Trim the inner border from this strip.

Refer to Borders (page 181) in the Construction Basics to measure, cut, and attach the borders. The strips are approximately 57 ½" for the sides and approximately 52" for the top and bottom.

5 Outer Border

Cut (7) 5 ½" strips across the width of the outer border fabric. Sew the strips together end to end to make one long strip. Trim the outer border from this strip.

Refer to Borders (page 181) in the Construction Basics to measure, cut, and attach the borders. The strips are approximately 61 ½" for the sides and approximately 62" for the top and bottom.

6 Quilt and Bind

Layer the quilt with batting and backing, then quilt. After the quilting is complete, square up the quilt and trim away all excess batting and backing. Add binding to complete the quilt. See Construction Basics (page 182) for binding instructions.

CHAPTER 9

MEMORIES AND REUNIONS

My mom's passion was genealogy. On our living-room wall, she had painted a huge family tree. It charted our family back for generations. I'd tell you how many, but to be honest, I don't know that I knew. There were enough that I never took the time to count them.

My favorite thing about that wall was all the cake that it brought me. Every person on the tree had their birthdate documented, and we would have cake to celebrate whichever great-great-grand-someone was having a birthday that day.

Literally every birthday . . . My mother loved cake.

One of the first times Ron came over after we'd started dating, we were having a party. "Oh, whose birthday is it?" he asked.

"Joseph B. Long's."

That didn't do much to clear things up, since Joseph B. Long had been dead since the early 1900s. I handed Ron some cake and gestured to the wall. "You know, he's some guy on the wall."

While I now know that Joseph was my second great-grandfather on my dad's side, I didn't connect that at the time. When I was a kid, and even as a new adult, I didn't worry much about where all this family history came from. I only knew that we had parties for the people on the wall, and I got cake because of it.

I didn't understand, but my mother did.

When you're connected to the past, you see yourself as a link. Her parties helped the next generation remember and learn about people connected to us by blood and history. There's a heritage of people who came before and the people who will come after. You take your place in the middle, holding hands with both sides.

My mom was a certified genealogist who spent her life telling other people's stories, and we don't have her story. Without sharing memories with the next generation, those stories don't stand a chance against time. They will disappear. They just go away.

My mother was quiet, friendly, and proper. She grew up in a society of tea and handbags. She was also a cheerleader and drummer. Does that surprise you?

Jenny and Josh teamed up to create the *Josh's Star* quilt.

Like most people, she changed as an adult. She went to school, married, and became a mother. Adapting to new stages of life, her bravery came in quiet smiles; her bold joy and outgoing nature disguised itself in humor and a desire to serve her family and others. I'm proud of the joy and strength I got from my mom. They've become part of my story.

My own family didn't know my story until I wrote it down in my first book. They were only familiar with my life from the time I became their mom until they moved out of the house. They had a smattering of knowledge from times before that, but it was bits and pieces. My origin story was new to them all. To them, I was Mom.

They didn't know what had inspired me to be a creator. They'd never known my dreams or passions. I wasn't any of the traits and characteristics I'd always held so dear. I was simply their mother. When I realized that, it kind of scared me.

The world is experiencing a chronic deficiency of stories. How many of us have really told ours? We have a past that goes much, much further than ourselves and a future that goes just as far. It's up to us to keep our history alive. We can do that with words and photo albums. We can do it with a quilt.

We call those quilted histories *memory quilts*.

Quilts can outlive us for generations, carrying our memories long after we're gone. I've rescued a lot of old quilts. I find them at garage sales and thrift stores. They're all beautiful, and I know they have a story, but I rarely find out what it is. That's why quilt labels are so important. They help tell the stories that could otherwise be lost. When you know something about the quilt, you know something about the connected generosity, relationships, and heritage of people who have long since disappeared. I'd love to find one that said, "Made for Aunt Mary on her wedding day in 1923." Wouldn't that be a treasure?

My love of stories and genealogy is partly why I always try to label my quilts. I document babies, holidays, and anything that has the potential to turn a quilt into a memory—just like my genealogist mother.

Recently, I made a picnic quilt for my granddaughter's wedding. On the back of it, I wrote, "Happy wedding day! Love, Grandma, Jenny Doan." I added the date in parentheses and wrapped it up for them. I hope that having the label documented there will make the quilt even more special for them.

People think a memory quilt is only necessary after you've lost someone to death, but a memory quilt can be created from the smallest detail of our lives. The most important part is that you're solidifying the memory. It's a way of showing love! Maybe your loved ones have clothing that they were thinking of getting rid of. It's something we all do—a resource that most of us have. Ron wears a lot of plaid cotton shirts, and when one gets paint on it or a hole and he's ready to get rid of it, I'll say to him, "Don't throw that out! We'll cut it into squares."

His ruined shirts go into a pile, and I cut them into five-inch squares.

When the kids found out I was working on memory quilts of their father, they thought I was being morbid, but these quilts will hold and preserve our memories. Our deepest recollections are set in our minds through our senses; every time I hug Ron, I feel the fabric of his plaid button-up shirts between us, smell his favorite soap, and appreciate the sight of him in his favorite colors. I'll be able to recall these memories every time I hold the quilt I make from his shirts.

I love that I'll be able to give those moments to my children as well. We may not wait until he passes to give them this gift of memories. Why should we? Memories aren't only for the end of life. Memories happen while we're smack-dab in the middle of living. They're steeped in emotions. They hold a blend of joy, pain, excitement, embarrassment, and grief. Lives happen in memories. They're created in everything we do.

When my children were young, they grew so fast. I would save all their old jeans and cut them into patches. I didn't make them as memory quilts back then, but even as little kids, they'd sit on those heavy patched quilts I sewed and get excited. "Oh, that's my pocket!" or "I know that button!"

I've decided to restore one of those old jean quilts, and I've done a fair bit of laughing. The jean squares were cut with scissors and sewn with a 5/8" seam allowance, as I'd learned to do sewing clothes. Some of the blocks are so different in size I don't know how I got them

Ella and Jenny with the *Elephant Appliqué* quilt.

together in rows and columns, but I did. Every time I unstitch a block, a wide seam allowance of dark-blue denim is revealed, protected from the same wear and tear the quilt top went through.

I had good intentions. I can still feel them woven into the old fabric and wound into the threads. It's a joy to work through a row of unsteady patchwork and stumble upon memories, or trim a particularly uneven block and imagine it set into the new quilt. I made those quilts way before I knew I was quilting. The edges weren't even bound. Instead, they were part of the old sheets used to back the quilts. I just rolled a couple inches over the sides and stitched it down on the front. Not a bad solution, but I want something different now.

These quilts were instant memories, part of our history as soon as I made them, and we used them for years. Taking them apart and reshaping the blocks, I feel like I'm honoring those moments. They served their purpose, and now they're serving a new one. They'll always hold and share the memories of our family. I value that even more than their ability to stand up to our many adventures.

Another form of memory quilts that I think we make without any real consideration is T-shirt quilts. We make them for our kids. Sarah likes to make them for her children as they graduate high school. Well, actually, she helps Natalie make them. Natalie is a T-shirt quilt professional. Last year, Sarah's daughter had so many shirts from school, sports, cheerleading, and church that they had to make two quilts! It spawned a lot of jokes that maybe Sarah should have slowed her kids down in all the things they did, but her daughter was so excited.

T-shirt quilts mean a lot to the receiver and anyone who knows that person. Every square is a piece of their history, a quilt full of living memories they can hold right now.

Natalie, Deannie, Jenny, and Sarah.

Almost by accident, I started my own memory quilt. One day I found myself with a pile of pretty, colorful fabric scraps on my desk. They were pieces from all the projects I'd worked on that day. I started stitching them together—tiny patches of color in random shapes—until I had a decent-sized patch of fabric, then trimmed it up into a scrappy little block for a crumb quilt. I have a soft spot for scrappy quilts, and I liked what I'd made. I saved that first block, and the next day I made another one. I'm still working on that quilt, making new blocks almost every day.

I create a lot of scraps, and I hate waste, so turning them into a quilt block felt easy—natural. I was several blocks in before I realized I was stitching my history. A fabric collage of my life. Bits and pieces of my daily projects sewn together in blocks. Because of that, it has a great deal of meaning to me now, and it continues to grow.

Memory quilts have two basic steps: find something that has meaning to the person you want to remember, and then get creative.

Someone you love may have a lot of ties in their closet. I once made a table runner completely out of old ties. If those ties belonged to your dad, you could get it out on birthdays or Father's Day and talk about your favorites or how he wore a tie every day. Can you remember which one he wore for your wedding? Or who in the world bought him the tie with the orange geese on it? Whatever the story may be, it's our job to hold on to those memories and share them with future generations.

A family I know who lost their dad brought me his shirts while they were grieving and asked that I make them into pillows. They wanted something to hold when they needed a reminder of hugging their dad. We made shirt huggers out of those sweet, familiar shirts for the entire family, even the little ones. As they grow up, the littlest of them may not remember a lot about their father, but they will know that they had a dad or a grandpa, and he wore this shirt, and he loved them.

Quilts can be made from outdated military uniforms to give family a piece of their loved one to hold when they are overseas, deployed, or even gone from this life.

My daughter's father-in-law passed away fairly young. He was probably in his sixties, and I knew him well. His daughter created little stuffed bears out of his shirts and overalls for all the children and grandchildren. They were things he'd worn daily—things that are part of the picture of him in our minds. It's hard to realize that some of the youngest kids won't remember their grandpa—his laughter and wit or his big heart that loved and gave without qualifiers—but they'll have that bear as a tangible object made of the clothing that once belonged to him. They might not remember his touch, but that fabric does. And those stuffed bears will create a memory of their grandfather for each family member.

It is a kind of magic that an object can cover the distances of time like that. Memory is a force to reckon with.

If you aren't sold on memory quilts yet, I have more ideas. There are quilts made with historical fabrics from linens that have been hidden away for years. There are I Spy quilts featuring wedding fabrics or baby clothes from one person or an entire generation of family or friends. There are quilts created with blocks coming from every member of the family. You can scan images on fabric, write with fabric pens, or sew on buttons and ribbons from favorite clothing or decor items.

Signature quilts incorporate a person's handwriting into the quilt. It can be written with permanent fabric pens or drawn in pencil and embroidered over. Either way, it becomes even more personalized to our loved ones. My granddaughter made me a signature quilt with all of my children's and grandchildren's signatures. I also made a signature quilt for my grandmother. I had people trace their hands on paper and write their signature on the handprint. Then I transferred the drawings onto cloth and made her a quilt.

The options are limitless, and I hope by the end of this chapter you have more ideas to bring quilting into the intimate details and memories of your life than you know what to do with.

I own an unintentional memory quilt that belonged to a dear friend of mine who passed away. It's made from the clothing she wore as a little girl. While using someone's clothing is traditional for memory quilts now, it's not why people used to do it.

In years past quilts and quilting were a necessity, not a hobby, and fabric was a precious

Jenny and Alayna with a quilt that Alayna made and gave to Jenny. Each grandchild's handprint is appliquéd on this sweet creation.

resource. People repurposed worn-out clothes to avoid wasting good fabric that could be used to keep their families warm. Money and memories were saved in the process. Looking at my friend's quilt now, the memories are an even greater value. Somehow, stitching memories together preserves them in a way that nothing else does. It holds the fibers together and gives the quilt a heart.

I am lucky enough to have two other very special and unintentional memory quilts in my possession. I started sewing as a teenager while my grandmother lived with us. Her art was embroidery, and she had a great talent for it. She would stitch floral patterns on squares of cut-up jeans for the same reason anybody else used the sturdy fabric—we already owned it. I don't know if she would have chosen something different given the option, but it was easily accessible, and I could always find her stitching along on a square of heavy denim.

After she'd built up a few blocks of embroidered flowers, she'd hand them to me and say something like, "Sew these together, Jenny. And can you put a little back on it to hide the stitching? I want to send it to Aunt Ingie."

Of course, I did. I was the only person in the family who could sew, and so it became my job to sew for Grandma. I assembled her embroidered squares into small quilts and wall hangings for years, sending them away to whomever she thought needed them. She used those blocks to share her love. That was a big part of the core memories I have with my grandma. It was service and time with a wonderful woman. I believe that working with and for her helped lay the groundwork for my love of quilting today.

Well, little quilts grow into bigger quilts, and after Ron and I married and moved away, my mom started sending me Grandma's embroidered blocks to make her a bed covering. (Back then we didn't really call them quilts, because we didn't know any different.) Even after I finished her quilt, my mom continued to send me Grandma's blocks, and I made more. By the time I was done, Grandma was having a harder time getting around and I'd finished several queen-sized bed quilts for my parents and siblings. Each came from the gorgeous, embroidered squares of denim that Grandma had made.

I made my own quilt last. Every time my mom sent a stack of squares to work with, I'd been able to save one or two of my favorites. Once I had enough, I put them together into a gorgeous quilt full of memories preserved in thread and color.

That quilt has *years* of treasured memories for me. I remember sitting with Grandma in her room when I still lived at home, watching her sew. She stitched her flowers on one block every day, as often as she could. After we moved away, I would go back to visit, and I'd sit in her room and talk and watch her sew. The jean fabric was stiff and difficult to stitch on. Grandma's fingers would turn red as she sewed, and she'd take breaks to stretch her hand and relieve the pain from fighting through the dense material.

When she couldn't push the needle through the fabric anymore, she used needle-nose pliers to pull it through each stitch of the embroidery. She made her beautiful designs using a bulky pair of pliers.

Those blocks were precious to me. As she aged, embroidering was one of the few things she could do that kept her mind active. She made so many squares we ran out of pants to cut up. So, I bought several yards of jean fabric, cut it into squares, and gave it to Grandma to keep sewing. When she put her needle into that fabric, her eyes lit up. The jean fabric was so much softer than squares cut from actual jeans.

"It's like sewing through butter!" she said. She was thrilled, and I was too. I only wished we'd discovered that years earlier! Thankfully she still had a long time to keep sewing. My grandma lived to be over a hundred years old, and she continued to sew almost to the very end.

My grandmother came from a family of seamstresses. They immigrated from Sweden to America, using their skills with fabric and thread to do so. I received that story and the second of my most precious memory quilts from my mother after Grandma died. My grandma's mama pieced it together with blocks of black, brown, and navy fabric from men's suits. As a seamstress, she likely had leftover fabric from her work and could have used that to sew together the dark woolen blocks. Or maybe they were remnants of worn pants from the men in the family.

Yes, pants! They cut up worn-out men's suit pants to make heavy blankets just like I cut up denim jeans to make quilts for my family.

But that's not even the most interesting part. As I looked over the quilt blocks, my mom pointed out that some of the squares had names embroidered on them. The story goes, she told me, that grandma's mama had used that quilt to teach her daughters to do handwork.

This was a practice quilt!

At some point in time, there had to have been more quilts that they made, but this is the only one I know about that is left. When my mom handed me this quilt and told me its story, it was like I'd found my link to the past. I felt so connected with those women. Through this quilt, I know my seamstress ancestors, and I carry on their legacy today. Their skill is mine, and mine is theirs. And I wouldn't know about these memories and history if they weren't preserved through that precious heirloom.

You know, I've had some century-old antique quilts given to me by friends—quilts from the late 1800s to the early 1900s. They were made by quilters who worked hard on something they loved. And I get to hold the work of that quilter.

You rarely see this today, but in those quilts, you'll sometimes find a small piece of a finished block with two or three seams in it. It's all the same kind of fabric, and not part of the design, so why did they do it? We assume it happened because the quilter didn't have a large enough piece of fabric to cut the whole shape.

Jenny and Talon filmed a quick and easy pillowcase tutorial in 2018.

The first time I saw a piece like that, it was on a small section of fabric no bigger than two inches across with three slips of fabric stacked and stitched together. I couldn't take my eyes off it. I wanted to touch it and memorize it. I almost tried to look behind it, as if I could confirm that there really were multiple seams back there. I felt like I knew the woman who had stitched it. She had painted a picture of who she was through her fabric and sewing habits. She was thrifty, using every scrap of her fabric. She was a little stubborn and a creative thinker. She didn't give up when it got hard; she figured out how to make it work. She appreciated art and beauty and had matched the fabrics and created a pattern that was more than utilitarian work. She probably didn't have a lot, material or otherwise. In this quilt I saw a woman who gave her all to do what she had to do.

When I look at that block, I see myself. What the quilter had stitched is something I would do in tight circumstances. I want to reach out and hug that woman. She did her very best, and by preserving that quilt, I can help her. Her work is being seen and remembered.

I have a quilt from the 1890s hanging on my wall. The colors are faded, but the seams are tight. I've often looked at that quilt and been amazed at how well it's held up. It's over a hundred years old.

Now *that* is an old quilt!

Then I had someone bring me an even older quilt . . . from 1867. That's over a hundred and fifty years old! It should be in a museum.

I marveled in gratitude that I got to be one of the caretakers of that quilt. Textiles can be fairly fragile, so when I see quilts like these, it's breathtaking. They're fading and have occasional worn spots, but they've aged beautifully. The thread hasn't gone bad, and although the batting may have thinned, the fabric has held its weave. It's an incredible feat for something made of tiny, individual threads.

Today, quilting is something we do for fun, but the process of quilting is what binds fabrics together, making them stronger. That's how they last so long.

Whether you quilt, sew, or are just curious about why people do, I hope you can see how precious your memories are, and how quilting can help you preserve that link between generations.

Holding the Link of Memory

One Mother's Day, I was out at my mom's grave. My son Alan and his three little boys were there with me. At the time, these grandsons were all younger than five years old, and they don't really remember my mama. My son began sharing memories of my mom, his Grandma Fish, so the little ones could get to know her.

After one of the stories, Alan's oldest son looked up at me, and in his little boy voice he asked, "Grandma, do you ever talk to your mom and dad when you are here?"

The fact that he knew we were there to talk to his great-grandma, and that she was my mama, tugged at my fraying heart. "Yes," I said to him. "Sometimes I do."

"Do you hear them with your heart or with your ears?" His little fingers had wrapped around my hand, and his eyes held me there.

I answered him honestly. "Mostly with my heart."

I like to think of myself as a fun grandma. I like to play games with my grandkids and teach them new things, tell jokes and have tickle fights. His questions opened a heartfelt conversation that I wouldn't otherwise have had with him. It was sweet that he cared. Even more, he seemed to recognize those feelings even at his tender age.

As my son shared more stories about my mother, this little grandson held my hand and extended the link of memories to our family history. I could almost feel my mother's smile. She lived on through me and my children, and the next generation of her family was ready and waiting to hold her close.

Aislinn, Isaac, and Jenny on set with the *Summer Stars* quilt that Jenny made for their wedding.

Memory quilts strengthen our family bonds by opening our hearts to talk about people and experiences of the past. When someone doesn't remember a friend or family member, a quilt gives others the chance to tell a story of a passed loved one. Along with the memories, a lot of love and therapy goes into making a quilt, and this all needs to be shared. When a memory quilt lives in your home, the stories associated with that quilt are talked about, and the memories and people find their way into our hearts. They touch our lives through shared stories and change us forever.

You can remember those who came before you in many ways, but you can't really wrap up in a photograph or a trophy. You can't replace someone you loved with memorabilia like old dishes, furniture, and perfumes or cologne that belonged to them. When a person passes away, many of their belongings are put in boxes or given away for someone else to use. You may pull them out every once in a while, but they always find their way back into a box. Those memorial items are often to be seen but not touched.

Quilts are special. They live on the back of the couch or the end of the bed. When someone gives or leaves you a memory quilt, or when you make one, you can literally wrap the memory of that person around you. When you miss them and you need to feel their love, it's still there in a tangible, soft, warm way. Smell and touch blend with color, creating a pathway to their memory. Think about the scent of a loved one's clothing. Think about the texture of their bedding, pillows, and furniture. Think about their favorite color. Put that in a quilt, and it will bring you softness and warmth, but it will also bring you your loved one. It's a memory you can touch. It keeps their stories going.

Our hands and hearts put these quilts together, infused with emotion. It's a tangible thing. There are many things that hold our memories. It's not a new idea, but a quilt carries it even further. It surrounds us with memories.

SIGNATURE
QUILT

C reating signature quilts is a tradition that dates back to the 1800s. Preserve treasured memories with this project, featuring handwritten signatures from dear friends and family stitched onto quilt blocks. Create a piece of history that will last a lifetime or longer!

Project Info

Quilt Size
73" x 73"

Block Size
8 ½" unfinished, 8" finished

Supply List

Quilt Top
1 roll of 2 ½" print strips
1 yard of print fabric for center
    squares
¼ yard of print fabric for
    cornerstones
3 ½ yards of background
    fabric (includes sashing
    and inner border)

Outer Border
1 ¼ yards

Binding
¾ yard

Backing
4 ½ yards for vertical seam(s) or 2 ¼ yards of 108" wide print fabric.

Other
permanent marker

NOTE: We chose to use a print backing fabric for our center squares, cornerstones, and quilt backing. If you choose the same, you will need 5 ½ yards or 2 ¼ yards of 108" wide print backing.

1 Cut

NOTE: Keep all squares and rectangles organized in sets of 4 matching like-sized pieces.

From the roll of 2 ½" print strips, cut:
- 24 strips into (8) 2 ½" x 4 ½" rectangles.
- 12 strips into (16) 2 ½" squares.
- 1 strip into (4) 2 ½" x 4 ½" rectangles and (4) 2 ½" squares. Add these to the pieces previously cut. You will have a **total of 49** sets of 4 matching 2 ½" x 4 ½" rectangles and a **total of 49** sets of 4 matching 2 ½" squares.

Set the remainder of the strips aside for another project.

From the print fabric for the center squares, cut (6) 4 ½" strips across the width of the fabric. Subcut a **total of (49)** 4 ½" center squares from the strips.

From the print fabric for the cornerstones, cut (2) 1 ½" strips across the width of the fabric. Subcut a **total of (36)** 1 ½" cornerstones from the strips.

NOTE: If you are using 108" wide backing for the center squares and cornerstones, cut (3) 4 ½" strips along the length of the fabric. Subcut (18) 4 ½" squares from 2 strips and (13) 4 ½" squares from the third strip for a **total of (49)** 4 ½" squares.

Trim the remainder of the third strip to (3) 1 ½" strips. Subcut a **total of (36)** 1 ½" cornerstones from these strips.

From the background fabric, cut:
- (25) 2 ½" strips across the width of the fabric. Subcut a **total of (392)** 2 ½" squares.
- (35) 1 ½" strips across the width of the fabric.
  - Subcut 25 strips into (3) 1 ½" x 8 ½" rectangles and (2) 1 ½" x 7" rectangles each. You will need a **total of (49)** 1 ½" x 7" rectangles. Set the extra rectangle aside for another project.
  - Subcut 2 strips into (4) 1 ½" x 8 ½" rectangles each.
  - Subcut 1 strip into (1) 1 ½" x 8 ½" rectangle. You will have a **total of (84)** 1 ½" x 8 ½" sashing rectangles.
  - Set the remaining (7) 1 ½" strips aside for the inner border.

2 Make Flying Geese Units

2A

Mark a diagonal line corner to corner on the reverse side of each 2 ½" background square. **2A**

Select a set of (4) 2 ½" x 4 ½" print rectangles. Place a marked square on the left end of each print rectangle as shown. Sew on the marked line and then trim the excess fabric ¼" away from the sewn seam. Press. **2B 2C**

2B

Place another marked square on the right end of each unit as shown. Sew, trim, and press as before. **Make 49** sets of 4 matching flying geese units. **2D 2E**

2C

3 Make Center Units

Cut a 4 ½" backing square in half diagonally. **3A**

Fold the long edge of each triangle and a 1 ½" x 7" background rectangle in half and finger-press a crease. Align the creases and sew the triangles to either side of the rectangle as shown. **3B**

Trim the unit to 4 ½". **Make 49** center units. **3C**

2D

NOTE: Use a permanent marker to sign the background strip in each center unit.

2E

4 Block Construction

Arrange 1 set of 2 ½" print squares, 1 set of flying geese, and 1 center square in 3 rows of 3 as shown. The prints in the sets should differ.

Sew the units together in rows and press toward the squares. Nest the seams and sew the rows together. Press. **Make 49** blocks. **4A 4B**

Block Size: 8 ½" unfinished, 8" finished

3A

3B

3C

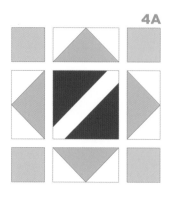
4A

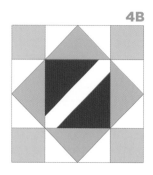
4B

5 Make Horizontal Sashing

Arrange 7 sashing rectangles and 6 cornerstones in a row as shown. Sew the units together and press toward the rectangles. **Make 6** units. **5A**

5A

6 Arrange and Sew

Arrange the blocks into **7 rows of 7** as shown in the diagram on page 170. Sew the blocks together with sashing rectangles in between each block to form the rows. Press toward the sashing rectangles. Sew the rows together with a horizontal sashing strip in between each row. Press. **6A**

6A

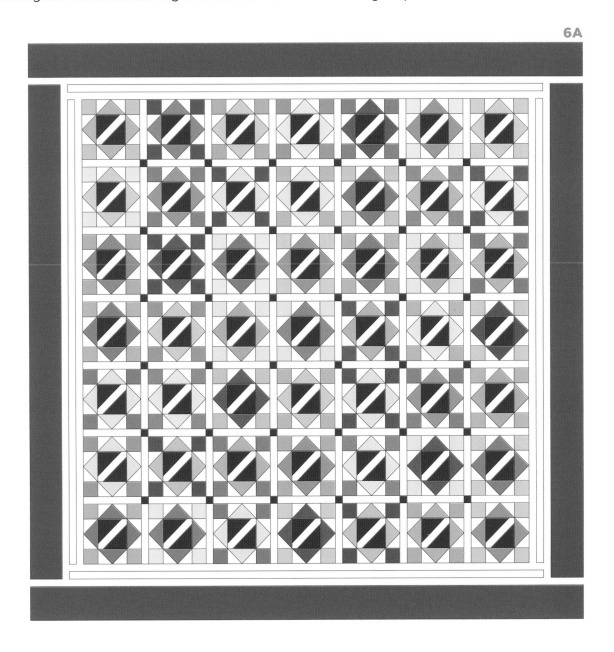

7 Inner Border

Sew the (7) 1 1/2" background strips together to make one long strip. Trim the borders from this strip.

Refer to Borders (page 181) in the Construction Basics to measure, cut, and attach the borders. The strip lengths are approximately 62 1/2" for the sides and 64 1/2" for the top and bottom.

8 Outer Border

Cut (7) 5" strips across the width of the outer border fabric. Sew the strips together to make one long strip. Trim the borders from this strip.

Refer to Borders (page 181) in the Construction Basics to measure, cut, and attach the borders. The lengths are approximately 64 1/2" for the sides and 73 1/2" for the top and bottom.

9 Quilt and Bind

Layer the quilt with batting and backing, then quilt. After the quilting is complete, square up the quilt and trim away all excess batting and backing. Add binding to complete the quilt. See Construction Basics (page 182) for binding instructions.

MAKING MEMORIES
T-SHIRT QUILT

've made more T-shirt quilts than I can count. I just keep coming back to them; they're so easy and so satisfying to create. I love T-shirt quilts because they're a great way to commemorate a special event or preserve cherished memories. Now's the time to dig through your dresser and pull out those tees you can't bear to part with to transform them into a cozy quilt that you'll love snuggling up with. It's the perfect way to recycle without feeling guilty. And T-shirt quilts also make thoughtful gifts that come together pretty quickly without piecing individual blocks. Create a custom quilt for a loved one and watch their eyes light up!

Project Info

Quilt Size
68 ½" x 83"

Block Size
12 ½" unfinished, 12" finished

Supply List

Quilt Top
1 ½ yards of white fabric (includes sashing and inner border)
½ yard of print fabric for cornerstones and star legs

Outer Border
1 ¼ yards print fabric

Binding
¾ yard

Backing
5 yards for vertical seam(s) or 2 ½ yards of 108" wide

Other
20 T-shirts
1 package of Missouri Star Sew Stable Fusible Sheets—42 Sheets
Missouri Star T-Shirt Quilt Template Set

1 Fabric Selection

Choosing the right fabrics to make the T-shirts in your quilt shine is an important step in the process. For this quilt, you'll need to select some fabrics to complete your quilt, and we're including some tips to help you make a great choice. All of the fabrics you'll need to pick out yourself are listed in the supply list. Any high-quality quilter's cotton fabric will do just fine.

The main focus of a T-shirt quilt should be the T-shirts, so selecting solid or blender fabrics for the sashing, inner border, cornerstones, and star legs is important. A blender fabric is a fabric that might have a small or subtle print that won't visually compete with other fabrics in a quilt. Pin dots or tonal prints could be considered blender fabrics.

The outer border fabric is a good opportunity to choose a print with a larger scale or multiple colors. You can even look to match a theme or color scheme to pull your whole quilt top together.

When selecting the binding fabric, remember that you'll only see about ¼" on the front. You could choose a contrasting solid or striped fabric to make a really nice frame around your quilt top. If you'd like a more subtle edge, you could use the same fabric for your outer border and binding to let the binding blend in.

The backing fabric is a great opportunity to use large-scale prints. Think about how you plan to finish your quilt and your quilting experience. Cuddle fabric makes for a soft backing, but it can be stretchy and difficult for less-experienced quilters.

2 Cut

From the white fabric, cut:
- (11) 3″ strips across the width of the fabric. Subcut 10 strips into 3″ x 12 ½″ rectangles. Each strip will yield 3 rectangles. Cut (1) 3″ x 12 ½″ rectangle from the remaining strip. You will have a **total of 31** rectangles.
- (7) 2 ½″ strips across the width of the fabric. Set the strips aside for the inner border.

From the print fabric, cut:
- (1) 3″ strip across the width of the fabric. Subcut the strip into (12) 3″ squares. Set the squares aside for the cornerstones.
- (3) 2 ½″ strips across the width of the fabric. Subcut each strip into 2 ½″ squares. Each strip will yield 16 squares. A **total of 48** squares are needed.

3 Prepare T-Shirts

Get your Missouri Star T-Shirt Quilt Template Set ready to use by removing the paper backing. Wash and dry all of the shirts you have chosen.

NOTE: If you want to feature more than 1 shirt per block, skip ahead to section 5.

After you've laundered your shirts, you can use your template set to judge whether or not each will be a good fit for this quilt. Simply lay the larger template over the graphic of the T-shirt you are considering and make sure that the portion you want to show falls inside the outer edge of the template by 1/4″.

Once you've double-checked all of your T-shirts and are sure they're going to be okay, trim off the neckband, the sleeves, and the hem. Cut the front of the shirt away from the back, leaving as wide a margin as possible on either side of the portion of the shirt you would like to feature. Keep in mind that we will be trimming the featured portion to 12 1/2″ square, so make sure the portion of the shirt you want to use is at least 12 1/2″.

4 Stabilize and Trim

The Sew Stable Fusible Sheets measure 14″. If you trimmed your T-shirts smaller than 14″, you'll need to trim the Sew Stable Fusible Sheets slightly smaller than your T-shirt square to prevent any of the adhesive on the fusible sheets from sticking to your iron.

NOTE: Never press your iron directly to the ink on a T-shirt. You can use a pressing sheet or fat quarter over the top of the shirt to protect your iron.

Center a fusible square with the glue side of the square touching the reverse side of the T-shirt square. Make sure your iron is on the Wool/Cotton setting. If you like, you can use steam. When you are happy with the placement, press down with your hot iron for 12–15 seconds. When you think the fusible square has adhered, move your iron back and forth to ensure the T-shirt and fusible square have bonded. Repeat to adhere a fusible square to the reverse side of all of your selected T-shirts.

Once the fusible squares have been bonded to the T-shirts, place the large template from your set on top of a T-shirt and make sure the graphic you want to feature is in the center. Use a rotary cutter to trim the featured portion of the shirt to 12 1/2″ square. Trim all of your remaining shirts. Set these aside for the moment.

5 (Optional) Use Multiple Shirts Per Block

If you would like to use more than 1 shirt per block, you have endless possibilities. All of the options we'll share in this section will be the same size as the T-shirt squares cut in section 3, so you can mix and match as much as you like without impacting any of the quilt construction.

TIP: When sewing T-shirt pieces together, go slow and pin in place if you like. A universal needle will work fine for sewing the T-shirts together, but you can switch to a denim needle if you're concerned.

2-Patch Block. To make a block that features 2 equal halves, cut (2) 7 ½" x 13 ½" rectangles from your shirts and (2) 7" x 13" rectangles from your fusible sheets. Refer back to section 4 for how to apply the fusible sheet. Trim the prepared rectangles to (2) 6 ½" x 12 ½".

Sew the 2 rectangles together and press to form the block. **5A**

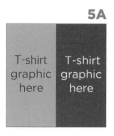

5A

> **TIP:** You can use the same-sized rectangles listed and sew them together with the seam running either vertically or horizontally. Use whichever orientation works better for your design. The block will remain the same size. **5B**

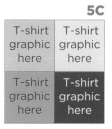

5B

4-Patch Block. To make a block that features a 4-patch design, cut (4) 7 ½" squares from your shirts and (4) 7" squares from your fusible sheet. Refer back to section 2 for how to apply the fusible sheet. Trim the prepared squares to 6 ½".

> **TIP:** The smaller template from your set is 6 ½". You can use this to easily trim smaller squares.

Arrange your 6 ½" squares in a 4-patch formation. Sew the squares together in pairs to form rows and press the seams in opposite directions. Nest the seams and sew the rows together to form the block. **5C**

5C

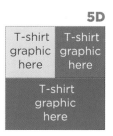

Split Block. You can easily mix the rectangles from the 2-patch block option and 2 squares from the 4-patch block option to make a split block. Remember that the orientation of the rectangles can go either direction. **5D**

5D

6 Make Sashing Rectangles

Pick up (14) 3" x 12 ½" white rectangles. Add a star point to 1 end of each strip by placing a 2 ½" print square on an angle (any angle) atop 1 end of the white rectangle with right sides facing. Make sure the print square is placed a little past the halfway point. Sew ¼" in from the angled edge of the print square. Trim ¼" away from the sewn seam. **6A**

Press the piece flat, then turn the rectangle over and press the print square over the seam allowance. Trim the square so all edges are even with the rectangle. **6B**

Pick up the scrap you just trimmed away and place it on the other side of the rectangle with right sides facing. Make sure the edge of the scrap crosses over the first piece by at least ¼". Stitch ¼" in from the edge of the print. Trim the excess fabric away ¼" from the sewn seam. **Make 14** sashing strips. **6C**

Repeat the instructions and add star points to both ends of the remaining white 3" x 12 ½" sashing rectangles. You will have a **total of 17** sashing strips with star points on both ends. **6D**

7 Make Horizontal Sashing Strips

Sew a rectangle that has star points on 1 end to a 3" print square. Follow with a rectangle that has a star point on both ends. Add a print square, followed by a rectangle that has star points on both ends. Add another print square and end the row with a rectangle that has a star point on 1 end. **Make 4** horizontal sashing strips. **7A**

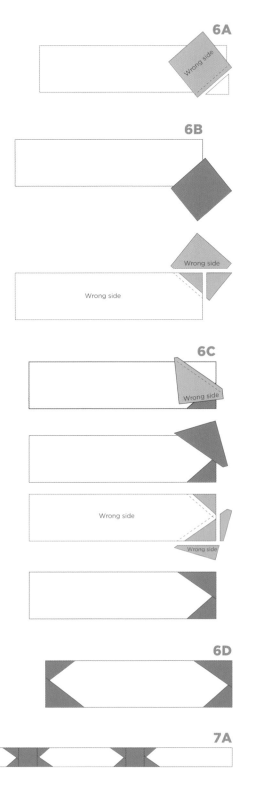

8 Arrange and Sew

Lay out the T-shirt squares or pieced blocks in rows. Each row is made up of **4 blocks** across, and **5 rows** are needed. Make sure any writing on the shirt squares is positioned the way you want it to be. Add a sashing rectangle that has 1 star leg between the squares in the first and last row. Notice that the star leg points in toward the center of the quilt.

In rows 2, 3, and 4, place a sashing strip that has star points on both ends between the T-shirt squares.

Sew the rows together, adding a horizontal sashing strip between each row to complete the center of the quilt. **8A**

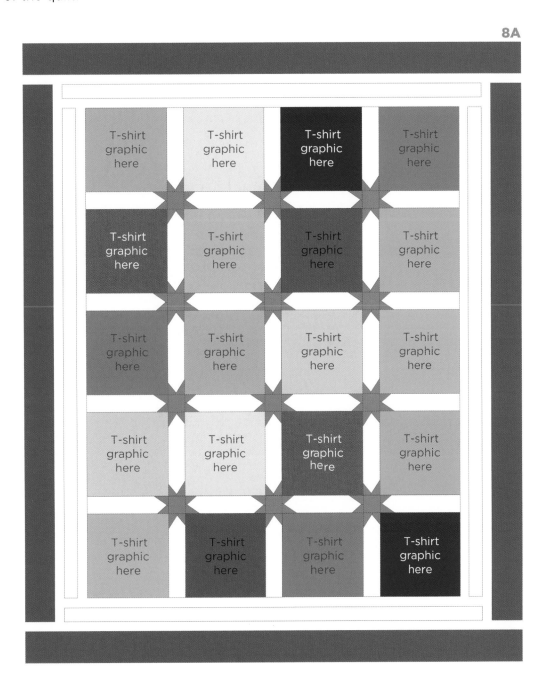

8A

9 Inner Border

Pick up the (7) 2 ½″ strips that were set aside for the inner border. Sew the strips together end to end to make one long strip. Trim the inner borders from this strip.

Refer to Borders (page 181) in the Construction Basics to measure, cut, and attach the inner borders. The strips are approximately 70 ½″ for the sides and approximately 60″ for the top and bottom.

10 Outer Border

From the outer border fabric cut (8) 5″ strips across the width of the fabric. Sew the strips together end to end to make one long strip. Trim the outer borders from this strip.

Refer to Borders (page 181) in the Construction Basics to measure, cut, and attach the outer borders. The strips are approximately 74 ½″ for the sides and approximately 69″ for the top and bottom.

11 Quilt and Bind

Layer the quilt with batting and backing, then quilt. After the quilting is complete, square up the quilt and trim away all excess batting and backing. Add binding to complete the quilt. See Construction Basics (page 182) for binding instructions.

A NOTE FROM JENNY

I have always believed that life's journey has a purpose. For me, it has been sweet and serendipitous. As quilting found me, my world and purpose blossomed. I've had experiences I never dreamt I'd be a part of. I've learned things that have nothing to do with quilting and many things that do. I've been blessed with adventures and knowledge I could only have because of the wonderful people I've met along my path. I've learned compassion, grace, and to give without expectation. I've learned to appreciate the talents of others and love the differences in what we all have to offer.

When I look back at my life, the most surprising part is how often I was made better by the quilts and quilters around me. My memories are tied to quilting. Memories of my grandparents, parents, and children. Memories of the quilts they've made for me and others and the quilts I've made for them. I still own the tiny four-patch quilt of my childhood. It sits folded in an antique chest but it only takes a glimpse to call up the memories woven through its tattered fibers. When I received my great-grandmother's quilt, it stitched her heart to mine forever.

As you look back through your life, the theme of your journey might surprise you too. It may be quilting, or it may not. Regardless, look for the creativity and inspiration that shaped your life.

It's the variety in our journeys that makes each of them so uniquely beautiful. We're creating lives of patchwork experiences, quilts made with color and nuance that no one else can replicate. Through happiness and heartache, embrace the milestones you encounter in life. These are the moments that will stay with you. They'll be both wonderful and heartbreaking. Cherish and celebrate each step in your journey as you quilt, and honor each one.

However this art comes into your life, I hope you let it affect you. Allow it to stitch up unhealed wounds, weave joy into the moments of your life, and pattern the steps along your way.

It's all part of your journey.

CONSTRUCTION BASICS

General Quilting

- All seams are ¼" unless directions specify differently.
- Precuts are not prewashed, so do not prewash other fabrics in the project.
- Remove all selvages. Press seams.
- Set the temperature of the iron on the Wool/Cotton setting.
- Set the seam by pressing it just as it was sewn, right sides together.
- Place the darker fabric on top, lift, and press back.
- Press seam allowances toward the borders unless directed otherwise.

Borders

- Always measure the quilt top in 3 different places vertically before cutting side borders.
- Start measuring about 4" in from the top and bottom.
- Take the average of those 3 measurements.
- Cut 2 border strips to that size. Piece strips together if needed.
- Attach 1 to either side of the quilt. Position the border fabric on top as you sew to prevent waviness and to keep the quilt straight.
- Repeat this process for the top and bottom borders, measuring the width 3 times. Include the newly attached side borders in your measurements.

Backing

- Measure the quilt top vertically and horizontally. Add 8" to both measurements to make sure you have an extra 4" all the way around to make allowance for the fabric that is taken up in the quilting process, as well as to have adequate fabric for the quilting frame.

- Trim off all selvages and use a ½" seam allowance when piecing the backing. Sew the pieces together along the longest edge. Press the seam allowance open to decrease bulk.
- Use horizontal seams for smaller quilts (under 60" wide). Use vertical seams for larger quilts.
- Don't hesitate to cut a length of fabric in half along the fold line if it means saving fabric and making the quilt easier to handle.
- Choose a backing layout that best suits your quilt.

NOTE: Large quilts might require 3 lengths. **A**

Binding

TIP: Find a video tutorial at www.msqc.co/006.

- Use 2 ½" strips for binding.
- Sew strips together end to end into 1 long strip using diagonal seams in the plus-sign method (see following). Press seams open.
- Fold in half lengthwise with wrong sides together and press.
- The entire length should equal the outside dimension of the quilt plus 15"–20".

Plus-Sign Method

TIP: Find a video tutorial at www.msqc.co/001.

- Lay 1 strip across the other as if to make a plus sign with right sides together. **B**
- Sew from top inside to bottom outside corners, crossing the intersections of fabric as you sew. Trim the excess fabric ¼" away from the sewn seam.
- Press seam(s) open.

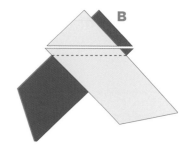

Attach Binding

- Match raw edges of the folded binding to 1 edge of the top of the quilt.
- Leave a 10″ tail at the beginning.
- Use a ¼″ seam allowance.
- Start sewing in the middle of a long straight side.

Miter Corners

- Stop sewing ¼″ before the corner. **c**
- Move the quilt out from under the presser foot.
- Flip the binding up at a 90-degree angle to the edge just sewn.
- Fold the binding down along the next side to be sewn, aligning raw edges.
- The fold will lie along the edge just completed.
- Begin sewing on the fold.

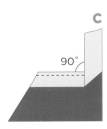

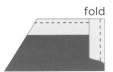

Close Binding

- Stop sewing when you have 12″ left to reach the start.
- Where the binding tails come together, trim excess, leaving only 2 ½″ of overlap.
- Pin or clip the quilt together at the 2 points where the binding starts and stops to take the pressure off of the binding tails.
- Use the plus-sign method to sew the 2 binding ends together, except this time match the edges. Using a pencil, mark your sewing line and stitch.
- Trim off excess; press the seam open.
- Fold in half with wrong sides together and align all raw edges to the quilt top.
- Sew this last binding section to the quilt. Press.
- Turn the folded edge of the binding around to the back of the quilt and tack in place with an invisible stitch or machine stitch.

ACKNOWLEDGMENTS

I want to acknowledge and to thank the team at Harper Horizon for pushing this project along and believing there was a story to tell.

I want to thank Christine Ricks and her team for their help and guidance in this journey.

I want to thank my daughter Hillary and her team for all their work and input. Hillary is a coauthor with me on this book, and she has an amazing way of putting pen to paper and being able to share the things of my heart.

I want to thank my children. They have taught me so much, and without them my life would not be the same. They are my source of inspiration.

I want to thank my darling husband, Ron. He is a constant support to me, and I couldn't do any of this without him.

I am so grateful for my faith and the knowledge that there is a plan . . . because I am mostly hanging on for dear life, and I couldn't do what I do without my wonderful fans, friends, and family who truly keep me going. There is so much joy in this journey!

ABOUT THE AUTHOR

JENNY DOAN is the smiling face of Missouri Star Quilt Company. Stitching together simplified quilts full of love and laughter, she makes quilting easier, more accessible, and friendlier than ever before. Watching her tutorials feels like coming home again. With over 750,000 YouTube subscribers and more than 225 million views to date, Jenny has sparked enthusiasm for quilting and warmed her viewers' hearts across the globe.

When she moved with her growing family to Missouri over twenty years ago, she never imagined that someday they'd have a successful quilting business. As in many small towns across America, employment in Hamilton was scarce, so in November 2008, on a modest budget, the Doan family bought a building in town and started Missouri Star Quilt Company. At first, they offered basic quilting supplies and machine quilting services, but business picked up when they started posting videos of Jenny teaching quilting tutorials online. From that time on her life changed forever.